Sorry,
Wrong Answer

Sorry, Wrong Answer

Trivia Questions That Even Know-It-Alls Get Wrong

ROD L. EVANS, PH.D.

A Perigee Book

A PERIGEE BOOK
Published by the Penguin Group
Penguin Group (USA) Inc.
375 Hudson Street, New York, New York 10014, USA

Penguin Group (Canada), 90 Eglinton Avenue East, Suite 700, Toronto, Ontario
M4P 2Y3, Canada (a division of Pearson Penguin Canada Inc.) • Penguin Books
Ltd., 80 Strand, London WC2R 0RL, England • Penguin Group Ireland,
25 St. Stephen's Green, Dublin 2, Ireland (a division of Penguin Books Ltd.) •
Penguin Group (Australia), 250 Camberwell Road, Camberwell, Victoria 3124,
Australia (a division of Pearson Australia Group Pty. Ltd.) • Penguin Books
India Pvt. Ltd., 11 Community Centre, Panchsheel Park, New Delhi—110 017,
India • Penguin Group (NZ), 67 Apollo Drive, Rosedale, North Shore 0632,
New Zealand (a division of Pearson New Zealand Ltd.) • Penguin Books
(South Africa) (Pty.) Ltd., 24 Sturdee Avenue, Rosebank, Johannesburg 2196,
South Africa

Penguin Books Ltd., Registered Offices: 80 Strand, London WC2R 0RL, England

While the author has made every effort to provide accurate telephone numbers
and Internet addresses at the time of publication, neither the publisher nor the
author assumes any responsibility for errors, or for changes that occur after
publication. Further, the publisher does not have any control over and does not
assume any responsibility for author or third-party websites or their content.

Copyright © 2010 by Rod Evans
Text design by Tiffany Estreicher

First edition: June 2010

Library of Congress Cataloging-in-Publication Data

Evans, Rod L., 1956–
   Sorry, wrong answer : trivia questions that even know-it-alls get wrong /
Rod L. Evans.—1st ed.
      p.   cm.
   "A Perigee book."
   Includes bibliographical references.
   ISBN 978-0-399-53586-4
   1. Questions and answers.   I. Title.
   AG195.E84 2010
   031'.023—dc22   2009051988

PRINTED IN THE UNITED STATES OF AMERICA
10   9   8   7   6

Most Perigee books are available at special quantity discounts for bulk purchases
for sales promotions, premiums, fund-raising, or educational use. Special
books, or book excerpts, can also be created to fit specific needs. For details,
write: Special Markets, Penguin Group (USA) Inc., 375 Hudson Street, New York,
New York 10014.

ACKNOWLEDGMENTS

My deep thanks go to my literary agents, Sheree Bykofsky and Janet Rosen; my excellent editor at Perigee, Meg Leder; Perigee's summer intern, Brian Sweeney; freelance copyeditor Candace Levy; my colleague Alison Schoew, who gave me some excellent advice; my friends Justin Gruver and Rob Stewart, who helped edit the typescript; and my good friend and extraordinary administrative assistant, known for her superlative word-processing skills, Robin Hudgins.

This book has been enriched by the hard work of many people. I am grateful.

PREFACE

Although most of us know a great deal, much of what we think we know "ain't so." We all harbor misconceptions that seem to make sense because they have been reinforced by other people who, like us, have accepted popular beliefs. Many misconceptions are accepted not only because they are popular but also because they connect well with what many people consider common sense.

It makes sense to believe, for example, that German chocolate originated in Germany rather than the truth: that German chocolate is so named because it was created by Sam German. Further, it makes sense to believe that Mercury is the hottest planet because of its closeness to the sun, even though the hottest planet is Venus, most of whose atmosphere consists of carbon dioxide, a greenhouse gas. Similarly, it makes sense to believe that buttermilk contains butter and that Danish pastry is from Denmark.

Not one of those beliefs, however, is true.

Although some misconceptions come from misnomers or misleading names, other misconceptions come from believing what appears credible in light of what is known. Indeed, many misconceptions are accepted precisely because they are plausible. For example, the more people know about Thomas Jefferson's political philosophy, the more likely they will believe—erroneously—that he wrote, "That government is best which governs least." Those words, however, were not from Jefferson. Although they were quoted without attribution in Thoreau's essay "Civil Disobedience," there is dispute over their original authorship.

Some misconceptions are so common that they are embraced by even cartoon characters. For example, in a particularly popular episode of *The Simpsons*, "Bart vs. Australia," Lisa tells Bart that toilets in the Northern Hemisphere (including America) drain counterclockwise, whereas those in the Southern Hemisphere drain clockwise. Lisa's confusion stems from misunderstanding the Coriolis Effect, the inertial force that deflects objects moving above the Earth—rightward in the Northern Hemisphere and leftward in the Southern Hemisphere (including Australia). Bart Simpson doesn't accept Lisa's conclusions, calls up Australians to find the truth about their toilets, and manages to create a diplomatic incident. Factually, it was Lisa, however, who was mistaken. Australian toilets flush in the same direction as toilets in the Northern Hemisphere. Although the Coriolis Effect can and does influence large bodies of water and air masses in the atmosphere, its influence on the direction of tiny quantities of water in a sink or a toilet bowl is negligible compared to the effect of the shape of the receptacles and the direction from which they were filled.

The art of debunking, though useful and enjoyable, requires good judgment. For example, although a tomato is, botanically speaking, a fruit (the ripened reproductive body of a seed plant), in most culinary contexts we treat it as a vegetable. Botanically, a cucumber is also a fruit, yet people who treat it as a vegetable in a salad are not necessarily unenlightened. Because tomatoes and cucumbers can, in some contexts, be treated as vegetables, it would be pedantic and obnoxious to condemn people for believing that tomatoes and cucumbers are vegetables rather than fruits. Debunking should, then, be done with discretion.

Similarly, in astronomical circles, Pluto no longer has the same planetary status it had before 2006, yet the reclassification of Pluto was not a discovery of a new fact but more like a verdict on facts already acknowledged. Schoolchildren who are now taught that Pluto is not a full-fledged planet are not, on that account, necessarily more enlightened than children of previous generations. The upshot is that those who seek to debunk misconceptions need tact, understanding, and, yes, humility. The beliefs of today's debunkers may be overturned tomorrow in the light of new or better evidence or evidence that has been more carefully examined.

Some debunkers, for example, take great pleasure in asserting that the Baby Ruth candy bar was not named after Babe Ruth. That assertion, however, is open to question. Those who make the assertion note that the official position of the Curtiss Candy Company, which produces the bar, has always been that the name of the candy bar has nothing whatever to do with the world-famous baseball player but was named after Ruth Cleveland, President Grover Cleveland's firstborn daughter, who had died of diphtheria in 1904, more than seventeen years before the Baby Ruth candy bar was introduced. Many people, however, including the researchers at Snopes.com, find it curious that a candy bar named Baby Ruth should be named after the long-dead child of a former American president and that it should appear on the market just when Babe Ruth had become the most famous person in America.

Why would the representatives of a candy company concoct a story about the name of an increasingly popular product? Fear of a lawsuit is one possible answer. Because the candy company had not gotten Babe Ruth's permission to use what looks like a form of his name, they might have been sued—successfully—by Babe Ruth. In fact, Curtiss did have to defend itself against at least one challenge to its name. A competitor, with approval from Babe Ruth, called its candy the Babe Ruth Home Run Bar. Curtiss, asserting that its candy bar was named for Ruth Cleveland, forced the competing bar off the market because its name too closely resembled that of Curtiss's own product. In short, there is reason to think that the Baby Ruth candy bar was named after Babe Ruth. At the very least, there is some reason for doubting the story about Ruth Cleveland. Had the bar come out in 1904, the year of Ruth Cleveland's death and a time long before Babe Ruth dominated the news, there would be no reason to doubt the official story.

This book, though informative, is designed to be fun. If you love trivia and pride yourself on being well informed, you should enjoy this book. If you like to engage in friendly bets, you may find this book profitable. If you like to discover the true or probable origins of words, quotations, and inventions, you'll most likely find much to interest you. Finally, if you like deflating the egos of know-it-alls, you should have ample ammunition.

I encourage readers to question and check any assertions made in this book. If you, the reader, enjoy this book, I shall be amply satisfied. If you not only enjoy it but also learn something, I shall feel useful. I created this book principally to entertain people. If some people also learn to question a bit more often, to be less sure of a few things, and to understand that even scientific propositions are correct only after suitable qualification, I shall be not only satisfied but also grateful.

Rod L. Evans

CONTENTS

Sorry,
Wrong Answer

Quiz 1
Origins

1. Where did India ink originate?

2. Where did Panama hats originate?

3. Where did the Norway rat originate?

4. In what country was Hollandaise sauce created?

5. Where did Dutch clocks originate?

6. Where did the polka originate?

7. Where did Chinese checkers originate?

8. Where did Danish pastries originate?

9. In what country did French horns originate?

10. Where is Venetian glass made?

11. In what country did Great Danes originate?

12. Where did guinea pigs originate?

13. Which nation invented vodka?

14. According to the evidence, where did French fries probably originate?

15. Where do Jordan almonds come from?

16. Where did French poodles originate?

17. Where did the ukulele originate?

18. In what city did the Harlem Globetrotters originate?

19. Where did Venetian blinds originate?

20. Where did tulips originate?

21. Where do diamonds originate?

22. What was the original purpose of what we today call an umbrella?

23. In what country did Russian dressing originate?

24. Where did coffee originate?

25. Where did the bagpipe originate?

26. Where did bullfighting originate?

27. Where did (sweet) oranges originate?

28. Where did pineapples originate?

Quiz 1 Answers
Origins

1. India ink originated in China.

2. Panama hats originated in Ecuador. They were shipped first to Panama before being shipped to their destinations in Asia, the rest of the Americas, and Europe. Many imitations exist, including those made in Hong Kong.

3. The Norway rat (*Rattus norvegicus*) originated in North China.

4. Hollandaise sauce, made after the manner of a Dutch sauce, originated in France.

5. Dutch clocks originated in Germany.

6. The polka did not originate in Poland but in eastern Bulgaria, from which it spread to Prague, Czechoslovakia, in the 1830s. The polka reached Paris by 1840 and swept the dance floors of Europe and the United States. In Poland, a variation did develop, becoming the familiar Polish polka.

7. Chinese checkers did not originate in China; rather, the game with colored marbles in a star-shaped board is a modern version of a nineteenth-century English game called Halma, which became popular in the United States during the 1930s. Although the game of Chinese checkers is played in China, it entered there from England via the United States and Japan.

8. Danish pastries did not originate in Denmark but in Austria. Inspired by Turkish baklava, Danish pastries derived their name from the Danish cook L. C. Klitteng, who popularized them in western Europe and the United States in the early twentieth century and who baked Danish pastries for U.S. President Woodrow Wilson in 1915. In Denmark and much of Scandinavia, Danish pastries are called Viennese bread.

9. French horns originated in Germany.

10. Venetian glass is made not in Venice but in Murano, an island suburb of Venice.

11. Great Danes originated not in Denmark but in Germany.

12. Guinea pigs did not originate in Guinea, Africa, but in South America's Andes.

13. Vodka ("little water" in Russian) originated in Poland, not in Russia.

14. French fries originated not in France but in Belgium. A gentleman of Liège named Rodolphe de Warsage, who was born in 1876, wrote of bringing home French fries from the shops where they were prepared. The delicacy spread to the north of France, especially to Lille.

15. Jordan almonds come not from Jordan but from Spain. The name is a corruption of the Middle English *jardin almande, jardin* being the Middle French and modern French for "garden."

16. French poodles originated in Germany, where the poodle was bred and trained to jump into water to retrieve ducks. By the way, *French poodle* doesn't describe an official type of poodle; those designations are standard, miniature, and toy.

17. The ukulele originated not in Hawaii but in Portugal. The ukulele is a slight variation of the Portuguese *cavaquinho*, an instrument that evolved from a small guitar called a *machete*. Portuguese sailors, in the late 1800s, brought the *cavaquinho* to the Sandwich Islands (which were renamed Hawaii). The Hawaiians called the instrument *ukulele*, from Hawaiian *uku* ("flea") and *lele* ("jumping").

18. The Harlem Globetrotters originated in Chicago. No players were from New York. The Harlem Globetrotters were organized in Chicago by Abe Saperstein in 1926. Saperstein chose the name *Harlem* to call attention to the ethnicity of the players and to persuade people to "think they had been around."

19. Although Venetian blinds were popular in Venice, they originated in Japan, where they were made from bamboo.

20. Tulips originated not in the Netherlands, with

which they have long been associated, but in central Asia. In fact, both the flower and its name originated in the Persian Empire. The flower is indigenous to Iran, Afghanistan, Turkey, and other parts of central Asia.

21. Diamonds originate from volcanoes, formed under extreme heat and pressure beneath the earth and brought to the surface in volcanic eruptions.

22. The original purpose of umbrellas was to provide shade from the sun. They appeared in ancient Egyptian, Greek, and Chinese art and have been around for thousands of years. True, some umbrella-like objects came to be used by the Chinese to protect people from the rain, but the first use of the objects was to protect people from the sun. When the Chinese used them to protect against the rain, they waxed or lacquered them.

23. Russian dressing was invented in the United States in the late 1800s or early 1900s. Some claim that the name came from the condiment's originally including caviar, a food associated with Russia. During the cold war, many United States restaurants called the dressing *sweet tomato dressing.*

24. Coffee originated not in Latin America but in Africa, in Kaffa, a southwest province of Ethiopia. In fact, etymologists link the word *coffee* to "Kaffa." Before Jesuit missionaries introduced the plant to Columbia and other parts of Latin America, Arab traders had brought the seed home from Africa and grew their own plant, known as *Coffea arabica.*

25. The bagpipe did not originate in Scotland, but it did become a national symbol there soon after it was first introduced in the fifteenth century. Pipes with a bag attached were written about in ancient times and were depicted in ancient Egyptian, Persian, Grecian, and Roman art. The bagpipe was used in Europe from 900 to 1500 and in the British Isles, where the Romans introduced it, during the early Middle Ages.

26. Bullfighting has roots in prehistoric bull worship and sacrifices, as when ancient soldiers in the Roman Empire killed sacred bulls in religious ceremonies. Indeed, bullfighting is often linked to Rome, where human beings would often fight animals in public contests. Some theorists believe that bullfighting was introduced into Hispania by Emperor Claudius during his short-lived ban on gladiatorial games. From Spain, bullfighting spread to Spanish Central and South American colonies and then to France in the nineteenth century.

27. Sweet oranges (*Citrus sinensis*) originated in Southeast Asia. Oranges got to Florida and California by Spaniards during the Columbus expeditions. Although oranges were cultivated in Florida in the sixteenth century, they did not arrive in California until the late eighteenth century.

28. Pineapples did not originate in Hawaii (where they were introduced in 1790 by explorer James Cook) but in the inland areas of Brazil and Paraguay. When European explorers discovered the tropical fruit, they called it *pineapple* (first recorded in 1664) because of its resemblance to what is now known as the pinecone. Originally, the English word *pineapple* was used to describe the reproductive organs of conifer trees (now called *pinecones*). The term *pinecone*, first recorded in 1694, was used to replace the original meaning of *pineapple*.

Biology

1. What kind of animal is a jackrabbit?

2. What kind of animal is a Belgian hare?

3. What kind of animal is a horned toad?

4. What color is a purple finch?

5. What is a titmouse?

6. After vampire bats bite hosts, how do they get to the blood?

7. How are cougars distinguished from panthers and mountain lions?

8. Through what body part do elephants drink?

9. What is special about a goldfish's memory?

10. Which African mammal kills the most human beings?

11. Where do gorillas sleep?

12. What is the longest animal?

13. What are most guinea pigs used for?

14. Where do most tigers live?

15. What is a sea cucumber?

16. Ornithologically, what is the difference between a pigeon and a dove?

17. Where do dogs do most of their sweating?

18. What color is your brain?

19. According to evolutionary theory, human beings descended from what?

20. Of these traits, having backbones or spinal columns, mammary glands, sweat glands, and hair and bearing live young, which one is not possessed by all mammals?

21. Which bird lays the lightest egg relative to its weight?

22. What is the world's most common bird?

23. What body part or parts do beavers use to tamp down the mud in their dams?

24. When polar bears are kept in warm, humid conditions, what color can their fur turn?

25. What will happen if you cut an earthworm in half?

26. Which animal would win in a quarter-mile race, an ostrich or a whippet?

27. What do dolphins drink?

28. Of mice, giraffes, whales, and human beings, which animal has the most neck bones?

29. What is the favorite food of mice?

30. What happens to a sea cucumber after it expels its vital organs in response to an attack?

31. What does it mean to call a horse a Thoroughbred?

32. What is the normal human body temperature in degrees Fahrenheit?

33. Why are flamingos pink?

34. What do salmon do after spawning?

35. What do opossums do when attacked?

36. Why are grizzly bears called *grizzly*?

37. What are horseshoe crabs?

38. Which mammal has the most teeth?

39. What are male sharks called?

40. What are female sharks called?

41. What are female chimps called?

42. What do porcupines do with their quills?

43. In what sort of climate do penguins live?

44. What is the difference between bulls and oxen?

45. What kind of fish is a sardine?

46. What would happen if you were to handle a baby bird that had fallen out of its nest?

47. What do lemmings tend to do when they are near cliffs?

48. What is the world's largest fish?

49. When opossums are in trees, what do they do with their tails?

50. What happens to a shark if it stops swimming?

Quiz 2 Answers
Biology

1. A jackrabbit is a hare (which, unlike a rabbit, is born with hair, is sighted at birth, and hops more than it runs; it has larger ears than those of a rabbit). By the way, Bugs Bunny appears to be a hare rather than a rabbit.

2. A Belgian hare is a rabbit.

3. A horned toad is a lizard.

4. A male purple finch is crimson, and a female purple finch is brown-gray flecked.

5. A titmouse is a bird.

6. Vampire bats get their prey's blood not by sucking but by licking the blood, much as a cat laps cream.

7. Cougars, panthers, and mountain lions are the same animal.

8. Elephants do not drink through their trunks, which are used simply to transport the water to their mouths; they drink through their mouths.

9. Goldfish memories last longer than three seconds, contrary to what is commonly believed. In fact, goldfish have been trained to navigate mazes and reportedly can recognize their owners after an exposure of a few months.

10. The African mammal that kills the most human beings is the hippopotamus.

11. Gorillas sleep in nests, consisting of bent branches woven together with softer foliage as a mattress. Although female gorillas and young gorillas prefer to sleep in trees, males tend to sleep on the ground.

12. The longest animal is not the blue whale or the lion's mane jellyfish but the bootlace worm (*Lineus longissimus*), a little under two hundred feet, making it almost twice as long as a blue whale and a third longer than the longest lion's mane jellyfish.

13. Most guinea pigs are used as food. Although guinea pigs are almost never used for vivisection nowadays, tens of millions of guinea pigs are eaten each year by Peruvians. Further, residents of Colombia, Bolivia, and Ecuador also eat them. Possibly 90 percent of lab animals are mice and rats; more rabbits and chickens are used as "guinea pigs" than are guinea pigs.

14. Most tigers live in the United States. Although there were tens of thousands of tigers in India a century ago, there are only a few thousand today. Some scientists estimate that there are fewer than ten thousand *wild* tigers on the planet. Note there are thought to be four thousand tigers living in captivity in Texas alone. What's more, the American Zoo and Aquarium Association estimates that possibly as many as twelve thousand tigers are illegally being kept as private pets in the United States. Although many zoos have tigers, people may legally own tigers in some states, such as Delaware, Maine, Indiana, and Idaho.

15. A sea cucumber is a marine animal, related to both the sea urchin and starfish.

16. Ornithologically, there is no major difference between pigeons and doves, though the larger birds tend to be called *pigeons*, and the smaller ones tend to be called *doves*.

17. Dogs do most of their sweating not from their tongues but from the soles of their paws.

18. Your brain is pink when it's alive. The pink comes from blood vessels. The human brain, if deprived of fresh oxygenated blood, will appear gray. Although about 40 percent of the living brain is composed of gray matter, and about 60 percent is composed of white matter, those terms aren't accurate descriptions of colors, though they do designate tissue of two different kinds.

19. According to evolutionary theory, human beings did not descend from either apes or monkeys but from a common ancestor of apes and human beings.

20. Of the properties listed, the only one not possessed by all mammals is that of bearing live young. Although nearly all mammals bear live young, monotremes, such as the platypus and echidna (a spiny insect-eating mammal), do not bear live young but lay eggs.

21. The bird that lays the lightest eggs relative to its weight is the ostrich, which, though it has the largest single egg in nature, produces an egg less than 1.5 percent of its weight. Although a wren, for example, is tiny compared to an ostrich, its egg, in contrast, constitutes about 13 percent of its weight.

22. Numbering more than fifty billion, chickens are by far the most common bird and, not coincidentally, the bird most commonly eaten by people. For almost three thousand years, people did not eat chickens but farmed them primarily for their eggs. Until the Romans came to Britain, people saw chickens as egg-providers rather than as meat. Chickens are thought to have descended from a pheasant native to Thailand called the *red jungle fowl*. At the beginning of the nineteenth century, chickens came to be mass produced. They were produced first for their eggs but were killed for meat when they were too old to produce enough eggs.

23. Beavers do not use their tails to tamp down the mud in their dams but use their teeth and claws. A beaver can use its tail and its hind legs together to stand upright, and it uses its tail as a rudder for swimming and as a warning device by slapping it on the water's surface.

24. Polar bears kept in warm, humid conditions often turn pale green—because of the algae on their guard hairs.

25. An earthworm, when cut in half, won't become two worms. It can survive being bisected, but the part that survives will be the front end, where the mouth is. In contrast, members of the genus *Planaria*, or flatworms, do become two distinct creatures when bisected or split down the middle.

26. In a quarter-mile race between an ostrich and a whippet, the winner would probably be the ostrich, which can reach, according to InfoPlease.com, about 40 miles per hour, whereas the whippet can reach about 35.5 miles per hour.

27. Dolphins don't drink but extract all the water they need from consuming food (mainly fish and squid) and burning their body fat, which releases water. If dolphins drank saltwater, they would upset their electrolyte balance and die.

28. Mice, giraffes, whales, and human beings all have the same number of neck bones—seven. In fact, according to current knowledge, only two mammals have a different number: a manatee has six, and a sloth has six (if it is a two-toed sloth) or nine (if it is a three-toed sloth).

29. The favorite food of mice is not cheese, but any number of things, including peanut butter, oats, fruits, vegetables, worms, and spiders. People who set mousetraps say that cheese quickly dries up and is, for that reason, less desirable bait than peanut butter.

30. After a sea cucumber expels its vital organs in response to an attack, it grows a new set.

31. A Thoroughbred (with an upper case *T*) is the name for a breed of horse, like Clydesdale or Arabian.

Thoroughbred racing horses are descended from three Middle Eastern stallions (two Arabians and a Turk) that were taken to England in the seventeenth century to be mated with British mares.

32. The normal human body temperature in degrees Fahrenheit is not 98.6, since the body temperature of a healthy person will fluctuate during the day and from day to day. People will commonly have temperatures of about 99°F in the afternoon and 97°F during sleep. Further, a woman's body temperature can vary according to what part of her menstrual cycle she is. "Normal" body temperature was first defined as somewhere between 98°F and 99°F. Because thermometers were calibrated by fifths of degrees, 98.6 was chosen as normal.

33. Flamingos are pink because their diet often includes carotene-containing brine shrimp and blue-green algae.

34. Most salmon, from Canada to Australia and from Siberia to Scandinavia, do not die after spawning. The exception is the kind known as Pacific salmon, located along the west coast of North America.

35. Opossums do not *play dead* if one means that they voluntarily pretend to be dead. Rather, when opossums are threatened, they *involuntarily* fall into a catatonic state that's convincing to their would-be attackers. The opossum's eyes glaze over; their lips pull back, baring teeth, and saliva foams around the edges of the mouth.

The tongue, furthermore, falls to the side, and the body stiffens, becoming insensitive to touch for several minutes or even hours.

36. Grizzly bears are so called not because they are grisly—that is, horrifying or gruesomely unpleasant—but because of their grizzled or gray hairs. It is true, however, that its scientific name, *Ursus arctos horribilis*, is based on a misunderstanding of naturalist George Ord, who formally named the bear in 1815 and misunderstood *grizzly* as "grisly," producing its biological Latin specific, or subspecific, name *horribilis* ("horrible").

37. Horseshoe crabs are not crabs but arthropods, more closely related to spiders, ticks, and scorpions than to crabs, which are crustaceans.

38. The mammal with the most teeth is a dolphin, which can have up to 260 of them. Despite those teeth, dolphins swallow prey whole and use their teeth only to grasp their food.

39. Male sharks are bulls.

40. Female sharks are females.

41. Female chimps are females.

42. Porcupines do not shoot their quills, which sometimes fall off; instead, when porcupines are frightened, their quills rise up to protect the animal from any perceived threats.

43. Although penguins (such as the emperor penguin) live in the bitter cold of Antarctica, other penguins live in colonies near the equator on the Galápagos Islands of Fernandina and Isabella, where the average temperature is between 67°F and 88°F. Some penguins live on the temperate southwest coast of South Africa, forty-some miles east of Capetown, where the average temperature is between 50°F and 70°F. Further, the Magellanic Penguin (*Spheniscus magellanicus*) breeds in coastal Argentina and Chile and in the Falkland Islands, with some migrating to Brazil. One of their largest colonies is in Punta Tombo, Argentina, where the average temperature is between 45°F and 65°F.

44. Bulls are uncastrated male cattle; oxen, in contrast, are castrated male cattle, especially those that are used as draft animals. (Steers and oxen are the same animals, though the word *steer* is usually applied to animals raised for beef.)

45. Sardines are not fish of one particular type; instead, they are canned fish of different species, though most commonly they are either young herring or pilchard. The juvenile Atlantic herring has also been used in a few places, such as Maine. Sardines are *packed like sardines* because the oil in which they are packed is often more costly than the fish.

46. Given that a bird's sense of smell is not particularly good, and that your scent wouldn't bother it, handling a young bird would not cause the bird to be rejected by its parents. Nonetheless, fledglings (young birds with feathers that are learning to fly) need to spend several days on the ground until they acquire the ability to use their wings for flight. Normally, the parents watch over the fledglings and fetch them food. You should usually leave fledglings alone so that you will not interrupt their development toward independence. Nestlings, which are fuzzy or featherless, should be placed back in their nests, if their nests can be found.

47. Unlike human beings, lemmings do not intentionally kill themselves. The 1958 Disney film *Wild Wilderness* presented footage that appeared to be lemming suicide. Yes, lemmings can be seen falling off cliffs, but they are frantically looking for food; food, as it turns out, becomes scarce when the lemming population explodes, as it does every few years in some Scandinavian habitats. In a mad rush for food, some lemmings successfully swim across lakes and streams and find food on the other side, but some, pushed by the hordes behind them, fall off cliffs into the sea and drown.

48. The largest fish is not a blue whale, which is a mammal, but the whale shark, a fish that often grows to a length of 40 feet or more and weighs over 30,000 pounds. In fact, the biggest fish ever caught was a whale shark that was fifty-nine feet long and weighed 90,000 pounds. Harmless to people, the whale shark eats only plankton. Note that the largest man-eating shark, the great white shark, is much smaller (20 to 25 feet in length) and weighs about 7,000 pounds.

49. Although opossums climb with their prehensile tails, they do not hang from them.

50. Although sharks of many species need to swim to breathe, other sharks can lie on the bottom and pump water over their gills to breathe.

Quiz 3

The Bible and Religion

1. According to the Bible, why were Adam and Eve expelled from the Garden of Eden?

2. According to the Bible, what sort of creature swallowed Jonah?

3. According to the Bible, who shaved Samson's hair, destroying his strength?

4. In the Bible, who is called Lucifer?

5. According to the Bible, what is the root of all evil?

6. What means of transportation did the wise men use when they came to visit Jesus?

7. According to the Bible, how old was Jesus when the wise men visited him?

8. How many goats were on Noah's Ark?

9. According to the Bible, how many wise men visited Jesus?

10. Where in the Bible is gambling specifically condemned?

11. According to the Bible, what did Mary Magdalene do for a living?

12. According to the Bible, what did God say to Cain after Cain asked, "Am I my brother's keeper?"

13. According to the Bible, how many times did Moses climb Mt. Sinai?

14. What makes a church a cathedral?

15. What is the *Day of Doom*?

16. Are Catholic priests allowed to be married?

17. Where will you find the statement "God helps those who help themselves"?

18. What role did Emperor Constantine play in establishing the New Testament canon—that is, the list of books regarded as authentic and authoritative Christian Scripture?

19. Why is the saddest and most solemn day in the Christian year, which commemorates the death of Jesus, called *Good Friday*?

20. Did Albert Einstein believe in a personal God, or was he an atheist?

21. What country gave as a gift the Spanish Steps in Rome?

22. What did early Christians do in Roman catacombs?

Quiz 3 Answers
The Bible and Religion

1. Adam and Eve were expelled from the garden not to punish them for eating the forbidden fruit but to prevent them eating from the Tree of Life and becoming immortal like God (Genesis 3:22–23).

2. According to the Bible, a large fish (not a whale) swallowed Jonah.

3. Delilah was not the person who cut Samson's hair; it was one of her servants.

4. According to the Bible, Lucifer was a king of Babylon (Isaiah 14:12).

5. According to the Bible, the root of all evil is not money but the love of money (1 Timothy 6:10).

6. Contrary to traditional legend, the Bible doesn't say that the wise men rode camels. They might have walked.

7. Contrary to popular belief, Jesus, according to the Bible, was not a baby and wasn't in a manger when the wise men visited. He was a "young child" and in a house. Immediately after the visit from the wise men, Herod ordered the slaughter of male children under the age of two. According to the Bible, Jesus could, then, have been about two at the time, certainly no older and certainly not a newborn.

8. The number of goats on Noah's Ark was not two; it was possibly seven but probably fourteen. Note that in Genesis 7:2 (King James Version) God tells Noah: "Of every clean beast thou shalt take to thee by sevens, the male and his female: and of the beasts that are not clean by two, the male and his female." *Clean* animals were animals that were ritually edible and included sheep, goats, cattle, antelopes, and so on. *Unclean* animals were ritually inedible and included pigs, camels, eagles, owls, snails, and so on. In the Douay-Rheims Bible, authoritative for Roman Catholics, the passage says: "Of all clean beasts, take seven and seven, the male and the female." It appears, then, that there were fourteen goats on the Ark.

9. Nowhere in the Bible does it say that exactly three wise men visited Jesus, though many people have assumed that there were three biblical magi because of the three gifts mentioned.

10. The Bible does not specifically condemn gambling or betting, though it does condemn the love of money (1 Timothy 6:10; Hebrews 13:5) and counsels against attempts to "get rich quick" (Proverbs 13:11; Ecclesiastes 5:10).

11. The Bible doesn't say anything about Mary Magdalene's livelihood. Contrary to popular opinion, the Bible never says that she was a prostitute. Apart from her presence at the Resurrection, the only thing the Bible says about her is that she was possessed by seven demons (Luke 8:2).

12. According to the Bible, God didn't answer Cain's question, "Am I my brother's keeper?"

13. The Bible presents Moses as having climbed Mt. Sinai at least seven times, though in the movie *The Ten Commandments*, starring the late Charlton Heston, Moses goes up the mountain only twice. As just stated, the Bible implies that Moses made at least seven trips. During Moses' first trip, God offers to make the Israelites a holy people. During the second trip, Moses accepts God's offer. During the third trip, God commands Moses to set bounds to the Israelites to prevent them from climbing the mountain. The fourth trip occurs after God speaks the Ten Commandments to all the people at the base of Mt. Sinai. During the fourth trip, Moses receives the commandments that form the book of the covenant. During the fifth trip, Moses is gone for forty days and forty nights, and receives two tablets of stone, which he smashes after discovering the Israelites worshiping the golden calf. During the sixth trip, Moses atones for the people. During the seventh trip, Moses carries up two tablets of stone, spending another forty days and forty nights.

14. A cathedral is distinguished not by its size or majesty but by its being the home church of a bishop's diocese or territory.

15. The *Day of Doom* is supposed to describe not a day on which everyone will be doomed but the Day of Judgment. *Doom*, in fact, derives from the Old English *dōm* ("judgment").

16. Catholic priests aren't supposed to get married after they've been ordained, but some branches of Catholicism, such as the Eastern Orthodox Church, will allow married men to be ordained. Before the Second Lateran Council in 1139, celibacy wasn't mandatory for all priests and other Roman Catholic clerics. Originally, and for many centuries, Catholic priests were allowed to be married.

17. The saying "God helps those who help themselves" can be found in Benjamin Franklin's *Poor Richard's Almanac* and perhaps elsewhere too but nowhere in the Bible.

18. Contrary to popular opinion and *The Da Vinci Code*, Constantine didn't create the New Testament canon at the first Council of Nicaea in 325 CE. The work of collating the New Testament books had been done over the preceding centuries.

19. The word *good* in *Good Friday* is associated with the earlier, archaic meaning in which *good* meant "holy," as when the Bible is called the *Good Book*.

20. Albert Einstein's religious beliefs have been widely misrepresented by both religious and unreligious people. He explicitly denied believing in a personal God but didn't call himself an atheist. Instead, he expressed a belief that the universe is in some sense divine (pantheism). In a letter to an atheist (1954), quoted in *Albert Einstein: The Human Side*, edited by Helen Dukas and Banesh Hoffman, Einstein wrote: "It was, of course, a lie what you read about my religious convictions, a lie which is being systematically repeated. I do not believe in a personal God and I have never denied this but have expressed it clearly. If something is in me which can be called religious then it is the unbounded admiration for the structure of the world so far as science can reveal it." At the same time, Einstein rejected the word *atheist* to describe himself. When responding to Rabbi Herbert Goldstein's question "Do you believe in God?" Einstein responded, as quoted in Victor J. Stenger's *Has Science Found God?* "I believe in Spinoza's God who reveals himself in the orderly harmony of what exists, not in a God who concerns himself with the fates and actions of human beings."

21. The country that donated the Spanish Steps in Rome was France. Begun in 1495 by the generosity of King Charles VIII of France, the Spanish Steps were designed in the baroque style and were given by the French to the city of Rome in the eighteenth century. Soaring up from the piazza to the French-built church and convent of *Trinitá dei Monti* in Rome, the Spanish Steps were thought to glorify the approach to the church. The steps are named after the Spanish and not the French because they are in the Piazza di Spagna, home to the Spanish Embassy, founded in the early seventeenth century.

22. When early Christians were in Roman catacombs, they were probably not hiding there to escape from persecution, but lying there dead because they were buried there.

Quotations (Part I)

1. Who originally said "Give me liberty, or give me death"?

2. Which American founder wrote "This would be the best of all possible Worlds, if there were no religion in it"?

3. Who said "Elementary, my dear Watson"?

4. Who originally wrote "Eternal vigilance is the price of liberty"?

5. Which American wrote "That government is best which governs least"?

6. Who wrote "He has achieved success who has lived well, laughed often, and loved much"?

7. Who first said "Consistency is the hobgoblin of little minds"?

8. Who wrote "Build a better mousetrap, and the world will beat a path to your door"?

9. Who said "There's a sucker born every minute"?

10. Which American politician said "I was recently

on a tour of Latin America, and the only regret that I have was that I didn't study Latin harder in school so I could converse with those people"?

11. Who coined the phrase "survival of the fittest"?

12. Where would you find the quotation "Spare the rod and spoil the child"?

13. Who originated the expression "Iron Curtain"?

14. Who originally said "Anyone who hates children and dogs can't be all bad"?

15. Who was the first to write "A little knowledge is a dangerous thing"?

16. Who said "I disapprove of what you say, but I will defend to the death your right to say it"?

17. Who originally said "blood, sweat, and tears"?

18. Who said "Every man has his price"?

19. Who was the first person to write "Music has charms to soothe a savage beast"?

20. Who was the first philosopher to assert "I think; therefore, I am"?

Quiz 4 Answers
Quotations (Part I)

1. There is a good chance that Patrick Henry did not say to his fellow members of the second Virginia Convention on March 23, 1775, "Give me liberty or give me death." We have no unimpeachable firsthand testimony that Henry uttered those words. Further, although both George Washington and Thomas Jefferson were present at the speech in which Henry was supposed to have uttered the words quoted, neither man ever mentioned the quotation in his writings. The words were reconstructed by biographer and U.S. Attorney General William Wirt from the recollection of two of Henry's contemporaries. Some scholars have speculated that Wirt might have gotten the words from Joseph Addison's 1713 play *Cato*, which included the lines, "It is not now a time to talk of aught / But chains or conquest; liberty or death." Note, finally, that Douglas Southall Freeman, in his biography of George Washington, said that it was his "thankless duty" to conclude that Patrick Henry probably did not utter the line for which he is most famous.

2. The quotation, taken out of context, appears to be thoroughly antireligious. Although those words look as if they might have been lifted from Thomas Paine's *Age of Reason* or one of Thomas Jefferson's anticlerical letters, they came from the pen of John Adams, who, despite his harsh words, saw religion as generally a civilizing force. In a letter to Thomas Jefferson on April 19, 1817, Adams mentioned reading some polemical books that reminded him of divisive religious arguments, such as those advanced by his boyhood minister, Lemuel Bryant, and his Latin teacher, Joseph Cleverly. Adams wasn't endorsing atheism, nor was he categorically denouncing organized religion. Rather, he was expressing frustration with hostile religious arguments. He wrote: "Twenty times, in the course of my late reading have I been on the point of breaking out, 'this world be the best of all possible Worlds, if there were no religion in it!!!!' But in this exclamation, I should have been as fanatical as Bryant or Cleverly. Without religion, this world would be something not fit to be mentioned in public company—I mean hell." In short, the full context of Adams's quotation shows that he thought that, despite the divisions produced by religion, religion is generally a civilizing force.

3. The words "Elementary, my dear Watson" never came out of the mouth of A. Conan Doyle's literary character Sherlock Holmes, though one can find the expressions "my dear Watson" and "Elementary" near each other in Doyle's short story "The Crooked Man." The expression "Elementary, my dear Watson" gained mass popularity in the movies, originally in the 1929 movie *The Return of Sherlock Holmes*, which starred Clive Brook as the detective and that contained in the last scene the words "Elementary, my dear Watson, elementary." The actor William Gillette is often credited with originating the phrase in the 1899 stage production *Sherlock Holmes*, for which he wrote the script and played the lead role. The phrase, however, doesn't appear in any published version of the script. Two things are certain: The quotation didn't come from A. Conan Doyle, and people nowadays associate it with Sherlock Holmes because of movies, especially those starring Basil Rathbone.

4. Although the statement about eternal vigilance and liberty sounds Jeffersonian, it appears nowhere in Jefferson's writings. Sometimes the statement is attributed to Patrick Henry or Thomas Paine, but it isn't in their writings either. The earliest recorded use of a similar statement was in the 1790 speech by Irish politician John Philpot Curran, who said: "The condition upon which God hath given liberty to man is eternal vigilance." Abolitionist Wendell Phillips, during an 1852 address before the Massachusetts Antislavery Society, said, "Eternal vigilance is the price of liberty." He later wrote that he believed that the statement was original with him. Phillips might have originated it, though the idea underlying it was as early as the 1790 speech by John Philpot Curran.

5. That libertarian sentiment sounds Jeffersonian, but it didn't come from Jefferson's pen. The call for minimizing government was quoted without attribution in Henry David Thoreau's 1849 essay "Civil Disobedience." Its original author might have been John L. O'Sullivan, editor of the *United States Magazine and Democratic Review*. The introduction to that magazine, founded in 1837, included the line, "The best government is that which governs least." John L. O'Sullivan, by the way, later coined the expression *manifest destiny*.

6. Despite the advice columns of Ann Landers and Abigail van Buren and the opinions of millions of people, that quotation about success did not come from

Ralph Waldo Emerson. Nor did it come from author Elbert Hubbard, minister and author Harry Emerson Fosdick, or author Robert Louis Stevenson, contrary to various popular beliefs. The author of those words is Bessie Anderson Stanley of Lincoln, Nebraska, who, in 1905, won the first prize of $250 and publication in *Modern Women* for her answer to the question, "What constitutes success?" Stanley's winning entry read: "He has achieved success who has lived well, laughed often and loved much; who has enjoyed the trust of pure women, the respect of intelligent men and the love of little children; who has filled his niche and accomplished his task; who has left the world better than he found it, whether by an improved poppy, a perfect poem, or a rescued soul; who has always looked for the best in others and given the best he had; whose life was an inspiration; whose memory is a benediction."

7. The first person who said "Consistency is the hobgoblin of little minds" was the first person to misquote Ralph Waldo Emerson, who said instead "A *foolish* [emphasis added] consistency is the hobgoblin of little minds."

8. Although the sentiment is Emersonian, those exact words are nowhere in Ralph Waldo Emerson's public works. In 1889, Sarah Yule and Mary Keene published a book called *Borrowings*, an anthology of philosophical remarks, in which they ascribed the following saying to Emerson: "If a man can write a better book, preach a better sermon, make a better mousetrap than his neighbor, tho' he build his house in the woods, the world will make a beaten path to his door." In his journal for 1855, Emerson did, however, write something like the quotation written above: "If a man has good corn, or wood, or boards, or pigs to sell, or can make better chairs or knives, crucibles or church organs, than anybody else, you will find a broad hard-beaten road to his house, though it be in the woods." That quotation from Emerson can be found in *Journals of Ralph Waldo Emerson*, 10 vols. (Boston and New York, 1912), VIII:528.

9. Although nearly everyone thinks that P. T. Barnum, the primary founder of Barnum & Bailey Circus, originated the saying "There's a sucker born every minute," nearly everyone is incorrect. Because there is evidence that the saying was used by some nineteenth-century American gamblers, it is difficult to identify any one inventor of the saying. The saying, however, can be indirectly tied to Barnum. One of his enemies did use it, referring to the gullibility of Barnum's customers in their readiness to believe in the Cardiff Giant, an exhibit purporting to be a ten-foot-tall "petrified man" that was a statue of gypsum designed to look like a dead giant. The man who uttered this remark was David Hannum, who was himself a charlatan. Hannum was one of a syndicate of five men who bought a statue from a man named George Hull, who had hired people to help him pull off a hoax. Some of the people knew what Hull was doing, but others did not, including two men who were hired by Hull's cousin, William Newell, ostensibly to dig a well on Newell's farm in Cardiff, New York. The two diggers found what appeared to be a ten-foot-tall petrified giant. Newell set up a tent over the so-called giant and first charged twenty-five cents for admission, and a few days later charged fifty cents. Archaeologists

pronounced the object a fake, and geologists commented that there was no good reason to dig a well where the "giant" was found. Nonetheless, Hull, the originator of the hoax, eventually sold his interest for $37,500 to the syndicate of men headed by David Hannum.

After the group moved the exhibit to Syracuse, New York, P. T. Barnum became so impressed by the crowds paying admission to see it that he offered $60,000 for a three-month lease of it, though in his memoirs he said he wanted to buy it. When David Hannum and his business partners turned down Barnum's offer, Barnum hired a man to model the giant's shape in wax and create a plaster replica. Then Barnum put the fake giant he had commissioned on display in New York, claiming that his giant was real and that David Hannum's exhibit was fake. When the newspapers reported Barnum's version of the story, Hannum was quoted as saying, "There's a sucker born every minute," to describe Barnum's customers. Although both Barnum and Hannum were perpetrating frauds, Hannum sued Barnum. The presiding judge told Hannum that Hannum could win the case, provided that he could get his giant to swear on his own genuineness in court. Scientists, including the preeminent paleontologist Othniel Charles Marsh, pronounced the giant a fake, and, on December 10, 1869, George Hull confessed to the press. On February 2, 1870, both giants were revealed as fakes in court. The judge ruled that Barnum could not be successfully sued for calling a fake giant a fake.

10. Those words about Latin America were not from Vice President Dan Quayle but were attributed to him in a joke by Republican Representative Claudine Schneider of Rhode Island, who was making fun of him. Schneider was in office between 1981 and 1991.

11. The person who coined the phrase "survival of the fittest" was not Charles Darwin but the philosopher and sociological theorist Herbert Spencer (1820–1903), who tried to develop the principle that all organic development is change from indefinite homogeneity to definite heterogeneity. Spencer invented the phrase "survival of the fittest" in his *Principles of Biology* (1864).

12. The expression "Spare the rod and spoil the child" is not in the Bible but in Samuel Butler's mock-heroic narrative poem *Hudibras*, published in the seventeenth century. The Bible (King James Version) actually says in Proverbs 13:24: "He that spareth his rod hateth his son: but he that loveth him chasteneth him betimes."

13. The inventor of the expression "Iron Curtain" was not Winston Churchill, who used it in a 1946 speech in which he said, "From Stalin in the Baltic to Trieste in the Atlantic, an iron curtain has descended across the continent." Rather, in 1914, during World War I, the Queen of Belgium said, "Between them [Germany] and me there is now a bloody iron curtain which has descended forever." Nazi Joseph Goebbels also used the phrase in 1945 to express concern over the Russian encirclement of Germany. In short, others had used the expression long before Churchill.

14. The quotation about hating dogs and children was not from W. C. Fields but from the teacher, scholar, and humorist Leo Roston, who delivered those remarks at a tribute dinner in honor of W. C. Fields.

15. The first person to say or write "A little knowledge is a dangerous thing," was probably the first person to misquote Alexander Pope, who said, in "An Essay on Criticism," "A little learning is a dangerous thing."

16. The libertarian sentiment about free speech sounds Voltairean, but it is not from Voltaire's pen. E. Beatrice Hall, while writing under the name of S. G. Tallentyre, wrote those words as a paraphrase of a sentence from Voltaire's *Essay on Tolerance*: "Think of yourselves and let others enjoy the privilege to do so too." Note that Norbert Guterman claimed that Voltaire wrote in a letter to M. le Riche "I detest what you write, but I would give my life to make it possible for you to continue to write." The letter, asserted Guterman, was written on February 6, 1770. In short, although the sentence expressed in the quotation ascribed to Voltaire is Voltairean, there is no evidence to support that he said those words or, more accurately, their French equivalent.

17. The first person who said "blood, sweat, and tears" was the first person to misquote Winston Churchill, who actually said, "blood, toil, tears, and sweat."

18. The first person to say "Every man has his price" might well have been the first person to misquote Horace Walpole (1717–1797), British art historian, author, and politician, who, in reference to a particular group of political enemies, said, "All *those men* have their price" [emphasis added]. He was expressing not general cynicism but contempt for a particular group of men.

19. The first person who said "Music has charms to soothe a savage beast" was probably the first person to misquote William Congreve (1670–1729), who said, in his play *The Mourning Bride*, "Music has charms to soothe a savage breast."

20. The philosopher who first said "I think; therefore, I am" was not Descartes (1596–1650), who famously used the assertion of self-knowledge as a fundamental starting point in his rationalist theory of knowledge, but rather St. Augustine (354–430), who advanced knowledge of one's own existence as a datum that cannot be overturned by those advancing radical skepticism.

Quotations (Part II)

1. Who first wrote "Power corrupts; absolute power corrupts absolutely"?

2. Please fill in the missing word to complete the phrase Kevin Costner (Ray Kinsella) repeatedly heard in his head in the film *Field of Dreams*. "If you build it, _____ will come."

3. Who originally said or wrote the sentence "We must all hang together, or most assuredly we shall all hang separately"?

4. Who originally said, in answer to the question why he robbed banks, "Because that's where the money is"?

5. Which American originated the expression "the forgotten man"?

6. Who responded to the question why he wanted to climb Mt. Everest by saying, "Because it is there"?

7. Who said "The capitalists will sell us the rope with which to hang them"?

8. Who said "A verbal contract isn't worth the paper it's written on"?

9. Who wrote "The only thing necessary for the triumph of evil is that good men do nothing"?

10. Who originally wrote "From each according to his ability, to each according to his need"?

11. Who originated the expression "nattering nabobs of negativism"?

12. Where will you find the expression "Lead on, Macduff"?

13. Who wrote the following and other statements extolling self-reliance and laissez-faire economics?

   - "You cannot bring about prosperity by discouraging thrift."
   - "You cannot strengthen the weak by weakening the strong."
   - "You cannot help little men by tearing down big men."

14. In *A Few Good Men*, what does Jack Nicholson ask Tom Cruise immediately before Cruise says, "I want the truth"?

15. In the film *The Graduate*, what does Benjamin (Dustin Hoffman) say to Mrs. Robinson (Anne Bancroft) when he asks whether she is seducing him?

16. In the 1967 film *Cool Hand Luke*, the officer called "Captain" (Strother Martin) makes a statement about a lack of communication between Luke (Paul Newman) and him. What exactly does the officer say?

17. Where did the phrase "Beam me up, Scotty!" originate?

18. Where did people originally hear the expression "Just the facts ma'am"?

19. In the 1997 film *Titanic*, what exactly does Leonardo DiCaprio say about being king of the world?

20. In *Casablanca*, at the end of the film Rick (Humphrey Bogart) says what to Louis (Claude Rains)?

21. Who originally said "Whenever I hear the word 'culture,' I reach for my revolver"?

Quiz 5 Answers
Quotations (Part II)

1. Lord Acton, a nineteenth-century English historian, didn't write "Power corrupts" but wrote "Power tends to corrupt."

2. The voice in Ray Kinsella's head doesn't say, "If you build it, *they* will come," but "If you build it, *he* will come." Although the referent of *he* was originally the baseball player Shoeless Joe Jackson, it later was someone who meant even more to Ray Kinsella—namely, John Kinsella, his father, with whom Ray plays catch during the film's finale.

3. Despite the widespread belief that Benjamin Franklin made the remark about hanging together as he signed the Declaration of Independence, no contemporary account attributes the remark to him. According to a popular anecdote, Franklin made the remark in response to a colleague who warned, "We must be unanimous. There must be no pulling different ways; we must all hang together." If anyone said those remarks during Franklin's day, it was more likely to have been Richard Penn, William Penn's grandson, than Benjamin Franklin. After all, the remark was attributed to Penn, the lieutenant governor of Pennsylvania and a strong supporter of the American Revolution, well into the nineteenth century. What is more, according to Penn family history and Philadelphia lore, Richard Penn, when told by his colleagues, "They must all hang together," responded, "If you do not, gentlemen, I can tell you that you will be very apt to hang separately." Still further, that version of the statement appeared in an 1830 book and an 1841 press account. So, then, why was Benjamin Franklin credited with the statement? An 1839 joke book and an 1840 biography attributed the statement to Franklin, and since Franklin was a much more colorful and accomplished man than Richard Penn, the story stuck to Franklin.

4. The quotation did not come from American bank robber Willie Sutton but from a reporter who interviewed Mr. Sutton in prison. The reporter received only a few unexciting, one-word responses, so he invented the phrase to spice up his story.

5. Although President Franklin D. Roosevelt often used the expression "the forgotten man," he did not invent it but adopted it from Yale sociologist William Graham Sumner, who, unlike President Roosevelt, advocated laissez-faire economics. Sumner was what has been called a *classical liberal* (libertarian) who opposed the Spanish-American War and the subsequent U.S. effort to quell the insurgency in the Philippines. He was a vice president of the Anti-Imperialist League, which had been formed after the Spanish-American War to oppose annexing territories. Sumner despised businesspeople who relied on government subsidies and contracts. William Graham Sumner's forgotten man was *not* a downtrodden person, overlooked by society but was a hard worker who earned money, only to have it taken from him or her to fund some social scheme.

6. The person who wanted to climb Mt. Everest "because it is there" was not Sir Edmund Hillary (the first to successfully scale the world's tallest mountain) but George Herbert Leigh Mallory, who disappeared on his last attempt to scale Everest in 1924 and whose body was found seventy-five years later.

7. The saying "The capitalists will sell us the rope with which to hang them," comes not from Vladimir Lenin but from the first person to misquote him. No one has produced written documentation of those words from historical records, though Lenin was said to have made the remark to Grigori Zinoviev, a close associate, shortly after a meeting of the Politburo in the early 1920s. The closest scholars can come to the original (mis)quotation is as follows: "They will furnish credits which will serve us for the support of the Communist Party in their countries and, by supplying us materials and technical equipment which we lack, will restore our military industry necessary for our future attacks against our suppliers. To put it in other words, they will work on the preparation of their own suicide."

8. The first person who said those words about an oral (spoken) contract was probably the first person to misquote movie producer Sam Goldwyn, who actually said of the famously trustworthy movie executive Joseph M. Schenk, "His verbal contract is worth more than the paper it's written on."

9. Nearly everyone credits the statement about the triumph of evil to Edmund Burke, even though no one can produce any reliable source for that attribution. Attributing the thought to Burke occurred as early as 1950 in the American press. President John F. Kennedy, known for quoting authors, liked to use the quotation and also credited Burke. In its fourteenth edition (1968) *Bartlett's Familiar Quotations* attributed the statement to Burke and cited a 1795 letter in which he supposedly wrote it. In 1980, in the preface to Bartlett's fifteenth edition, the editors admitted that they were incorrect. Despite diligent investigation, no researcher has ever found the origin of those exact words in Burke or anyone else. In short, the original author of those words remains unknown.

10. The first person to say "From each according to his ability, to each according to his need" was not Karl Marx but the first person to misquote Marx's own statements, which were from his *Critique of the Gotha Program* and not from the *Communist Manifesto*. Marx was himself paraphrasing a quotation from French historian and politician Louis Blanc, who said: "Let each produce according to his aptitudes and his force; let each consume according to his need."

11. Speechwriter and author William Safire invented the phrase "nattering nabobs of negativism," though Spiro Agnew, President Nixon's vice president, made those words famous . . . or infamous.

12. In *Macbeth*, the quotation isn't "Lead on Macduff" but "Lay on, Macduff, and damned be him who first cries 'Hold! Enough!'" Macbeth is telling his nemesis Macduff that he intends to fight, not to yield; in other words, Macbeth is challenging Macduff to attack ("lay on"). Macduff kills Macbeth.

13. Although the individualistic sayings extolling self-reliance have commonly been ascribed to President Lincoln, they weren't from him. So common is the belief that the sayings came from Lincoln that President Reagan, in a speech he gave at the 1992 Republican convention in Houston, credited the words to Abe. In reality, the words came from the pen of William John Henry Boetcker (1873–1962), a German-born American minister and motivational speaker. An outspoken political conservative, the Reverend Boetcker is remembered for his pamphlet "The Ten Carrots." Originally published in 1916, "The Ten Carrots" came to be ascribed to Lincoln in 1942, when Boetcker's maxims and some Lincoln material were printed on a leaflet by a conservative political organization called the Committee for Constitutional Government. Although Boetcker's maxims were on the opposite side of the Lincoln material, some people, knowingly or unknowingly, came to ascribe all the material to Lincoln. Eventually, increasing numbers of people came to believe that Lincoln had written "The Ten Carrots." The leaflet bore the title "Lincoln on Limitations," though Boetcker's name was printed on the side presenting "The Ten Carrots." There are several minor variants of the pamphlet in circulation, but the most popular version is as follows:

- You cannot bring about prosperity by discouraging thrift.
- You cannot strengthen the weak by weakening the strong.

- You cannot help little men by tearing down big men.
- You cannot lift the wage earner by pulling down the wage payer.
- You cannot help the poor by destroying the rich.
- You cannot establish sound security on borrowed money.
- You cannot further the brotherhood of man by inciting class hatred.
- You cannot keep out of trouble by spending more than you earn.
- You cannot build character and courage by destroying men's initiative and independence.
- And you cannot help men permanently by doing for them what they can and should do for themselves.

14. Nicholson, in *A Few Good Men*, doesn't say, "You want the truth?" Instead, he says, "You want answers?" Then Cruise says, "I want the truth!" Whereupon Nicholson shouts, "You can't handle the truth!"

15. Contrary to popular opinion, Benjamin does not say, "Mrs. Robinson, are you trying to seduce me?" Instead, he actually says, "Mrs. Robinson, you're trying to seduce me. Aren't you?"

16. Contrary to popular opinion, the officer doesn't say, "What we have here is a failure to communicate." Instead, he actually says, "What we've got here is [pause] failure to communicate."

17. Although the phrase "Beam me up, Scotty!" is a catchphrase indissolubly linked with the TV series *Star Trek*, it was never uttered in any *Star Trek* TV episode or movie. One can, however, find similar expressions. For example, in the 1986 movie *Star Trek IV: The Voyage Home*, Captain Kirk says, "Beam me up, Mr. Scott." Kirk also says, "Scotty, beam us up" in "The Gamesters of Triskelion," a second-season episode from the original series first broadcast on January 5, 1968. Further, Kirk says, "Beam us up, Scotty" in *Star Trek: The Animated Series* in the episodes "The Lorelei Signal" and "The Infinite Vulcan." Finally, in the 1994 movie *Star Trek Generations*, Kirk says, "Beam them out of there, Scotty." The complete phrase was eventually uttered by William Shatner not in a movie or TV series but in the audio adaptation of his novel *Star Trek: The Ashes of Eden*. Later, the actor who played Scotty, James Doohan, chose the phrase as the title of his autobiography.

18. Although "Just the facts, ma'am" came to be known as the catchphrase for TV's *Dragnet*, it was never uttered by Joe Friday on the show. The closest Friday (Jack Webb) came to the phrase occurred when he said, "All we want are the facts, ma'am" and "All we know are the facts, ma'am." There was, however, a short audio satire released on September 21, 1953, as a 45-rpm single called "St. George and the Dragonet" that did use the famous phrase. The script was written by Stan Freberg and Daws Butler (the voice of Yogi Bear, Quick Draw McGraw, Snagglepuss, and Huckleberry Hound).

19. Leonardo DiCaprio says, "I'm the king of the world," not "I'm king of the world."

20. Rick (Bogart) doesn't say, "This could be the beginning of a beautiful friendship," or "I think this is the start of a beautiful friendship." Instead, he actually says, "Louis, I think this is the beginning of a beautiful friendship."

21. Although the statement about reaching for a revolver is uncivilized enough to have come from Nazi Hermann Goering, to whom it is usually attributed, a version of it actually comes from playwright Hanns Johst's drama *Schlageter*, an expression of Nazi ideology performed on Hitler's birthday to celebrate his appointment to chancellor. The play was a heroic biography of the proto-Nazi martyr Albert Leo Schlageter. It was produced at the State Playhouse in Berlin in 1933, the year Hitler came to power. The original line, in English, would be: "When I hear of culture / hear the word 'culture' . . . I release the safety catch of my Browning!" (Act 1, Scene 1). In German: "Wenn ich Kultur höre . . . entsichere ich meinen Browning!" The line is spoken by another character talking with the young Schlageter.

Geography

1. Where was the first European settlement in New England?

2. What is Big Ben in London?

3. What is Florida's westernmost key?

4. What is the easternmost state in the United States?

5. If you were in the United States and dug a hole until you ended up on the other side of the world, where would you be?

6. How many directions are there at the North Pole?

7. Where is Scotland Yard?

8. New York's East River is technically what sort of body of water?

9. What is the largest desert?

10. Of Nevada and Illinois, which state is west of the Mississippi River?

11. Where is Yellowstone Park?

12. What part of the world today would be equivalent to ancient Gaul?

13. In what continent is Moscow?

14. Excluding cities in Alaska, which U.S. city is the largest in area?

15. Which is farther west, Reno, Nevada, or Los Angeles, California?

16. If you head due south from Detroit, Michigan, what will be the first foreign country you enter?

17. What is the official name of America's state that is the smallest in area?

18. Which is the largest lake completely in Canada?

19. Traditionally, a British hamlet was distinguished from other villages by what feature?

20. Which is the world's largest lake?

21. What is the world's longest railroad tunnel?

22. The island of Elba, to which Napoleon I was banished in 1814, lies off the coast of Italy in what sea?

23. On what continent will one find Vinson Massif, its tallest mountain?

24. True or false: Prague is east of Vienna.

25. True or false: Alaska's Near Islands in the Aleutians are west of Wellington, New Zealand.

26. If you're in Calais, Maine, are you closer to San Diego, California, or Dublin, Ireland?

27. True or false: The Atlantic end of the Panama Canal is west of the Pacific end.

28. What is Great Britain?

29. What is the deepest gorge in the United States?

30. Of Suriname, Gabon, Guinea, Mauritania, and Senegal, which country *isn't* in Africa?

31. What is Hong Kong?

32. Where would one find Death Valley?

33. In what body of water is Bermuda?

34. How many cities in California are called "Hollywood"?

35. Of London, Dallas, and Washington, DC, which city has the lowest average annual precipitation?

36. In what city is the Pentagon?

37. Which U.S. states are located partly or wholly north of the southernmost piece of Canada, including Pelee Island?

38. In what part of the United States did the practice of branding cattle begin?

39. Where is the Sierra Nevada mountain range?

40. What is the largest non-Alaskan national park in the United States?

41. What continent has the highest average elevation?

42. What is the difference between the Netherlands and Holland?

43. From what ocean does the Panama Canal receive water?

44. In what United States city was the first skyscraper built?

45. What is the world's largest lake in surface area rather than in volume?

46. What is the largest sand desert?

47. What is the largest city park in the United States?

48. Where is most of the gold stored in the United States held?

49. Where are the Plains of Abraham?

50. In 1836, the Battle of the Alamo was fought over what territory?

Quiz 6 Answers
Geography

1. The first European settlement in New England was not Plymouth, Massachusetts, in 1620 but near the mouth of the Kennebec River in Maine in 1607 (in present-day Phippsburg) under the leadership of George Popham. It did not last more than a year, though, because of a hard winter and the death of the colony's chief sponsors.

2. Big Ben is not the clock but the largest bell in the clock, named after Sir Benjamin Hall, the commissioner of works in 1859 when the bell was installed.

3. Florida's westernmost key is not Key West because the Marquesas Keys are west of Key West; the Dry Tortugas, home of the Fort Jefferson National Monument, are west of the Marquesas Keys. In short, the Dry Tortugas are Florida's westernmost keys.

4. The easternmost state in the United States is not Maine but Alaska, some of whose Aleutian Islands (the Rat Islands and the Near Islands) lie west of the eightieth meridian, which divides the Eastern and Western Hemispheres.

5. A hole dug in the United States until it reaches the other side would lead not to China but to an area in the Indian Ocean west of Australia and east of South Africa. Note that both the United States and China are in the Northern Hemisphere.

6. There is only one direction at the North Pole—south.

7. Scotland Yard is in England.

8. New York's East River is technically a tidal strait.

9. The largest desert is Antarctica, known as a cold desert. Sand and heat are not essential to deserts. What defines a desert is the amount of precipitation (under ten inches yearly).

10. Both Nevada and a small part of Illinois lie west of the Mississippi River, because Kaskaskia, Illinois, has been west of the Mississippi since a nineteenth-century flood caused the river to cut itself a new channel.

11. Yellowstone Park is in not only Wyoming but also parts of Montana and Idaho.

12. In today's world, Gaul would describe not only France but also two regions that were inhabited by the Celts: Gallia Cisalpina, or northern Italy, and Gallia Transalpina, the area roughly equivalent to present-day France, including parts of Belgium, Germany, Switzerland, and the Netherlands.

13. Moscow is in Europe.

14. Excluding Alaskan cities, the largest United States city is not Los Angeles (469.1 square miles, according to *The World Almanac and Book of Facts* 2009) but Jacksonville, Florida (757.7 square miles), which is larger than not only Los Angeles but also Oklahoma City, Houston, and Phoenix.

15. Reno, Nevada, is farther west than Los Angeles, California.

16. If you headed due south from Detroit, Michigan, the first foreign country you would enter would be Canada.

17. The U.S. state that is the smallest in area is called Rhode Island and Providence Plantations. Ironically, the smallest state has the largest official name.

18. The largest lake completely in Canada is Great Bear Lake. Although Superior and Huron are larger than Great Bear Lake, neither is entirely inside Canada. What's more, Great Bear Lake, in the Northwest Territories, has a total area of more than nineteen thousand square miles, making it larger than the Canadian portions of Lake Superior, Lake Erie, and Lake Ontario.

19. A British hamlet was without a church of its own.

20. The world's largest lake is the Caspian Sea (143,244 square miles, according to *The World Almanac and Book of Facts* 2009), though Lake Superior is the largest freshwater lake.

21. The world's longest railroad tunnel is not the Channel Tunnel (the Chunnel), which stretches over 31 miles between Cheriton in Kent, England, and Sangatte in northern France. Rather, the world's longest railroad tunnel is the Seikan Tunnel between the Japanese islands of Honshu and Hokkaido; it spans an impressive 33.46 miles. The Chunnel, however, is the world's longest *underwater* tunnel, because it runs 24 miles under the channel. "Only" 14.5 miles of the Seikan Tunnel are underwater.

22. Elba lies off the Italian coast in the Tyrrhenian Sea.

23. The mountain Vinson Massif is in Antarctica.

24. The answer is false; Prague is not east but west of Vienna.

25. The answer is true; Alaska's Near Islands in the Aleutians are west of Wellington, New Zealand.

26. If you are in Calais, Maine, you are closer to Dublin, Ireland, than you are to San Diego, California. By the way, *Calais* (the name of the city in Maine) sounds like *callus/callous*.

27. The answer is true; the Atlantic end of the Panama Canal is, in fact, west of the Pacific end.

28. Great Britain is the largest of the British Isles; it comprises England, Scotland, and Wales.

29. The deepest gorge in the United States is not the Grand Canyon but Hells Canyon of the Snake River between Idaho and Oregon. It is about 7,900 feet deep, about half a mile deeper than the Grand Canyon. The comparison between the two, however, may not be quite

fair because the Grand Canyon is a huge hole in the surrounding plateau, whereas Hells Canyon is in mountain-
ous country.

30. Of the countries listed, the only one not in Africa
is Suriname, a republic on the northeast coast of South
America; it was once a territory of the Netherlands.

31. Technically, Hong Kong is not a city but a "special
administrative region" of the People's Republic of China.
Hong Kong contains many islands and cities within it,
such as Kowloon, Sha Tin New Town, and Victoria City,
which is located on Hong Kong Island. Central District,
where the tall buildings are located, is on the northern
shore of Hong Kong Island.

32. Death Valley is in both California and Nevada.

33. Bermuda is not in the Caribbean but the Atlantic
Ocean, 570 to 580 miles east of Cape Hatteras, North
Carolina, and about 1,000 miles north of the Caribbean Sea. Bermuda is not just one island but about three
hundred islets. Its weather is moderate because of
exposure to the warm Gulf Stream. The temperature in
Bermuda ranges from 63°F in the winter to 79°F in the
summer.

34. There are no cities in California called "Hollywood."
Hollywood is a district of Los Angeles. An area that is
now part of Los Angeles was settled in the 1880s and
named "Hollywood" in 1887 by Mrs. Horace H. Wilcox,
wife of an early developer. In 1903, Hollywood was incor-
porated as a city. In 1910, the residents voted to become

part of Los Angeles, and that has been the area's status ever since.

35. According to WeatherBase.com, London's average annual precipitation is 29.7 inches, Dallas's is 33.3 inches, and Washington, DC's is 39.3 inches, making London the city with the least annual precipitation of the three.

36. The Pentagon is in Arlington, Virginia.

37. There are twenty-seven U.S. states located partly or wholly north of the southernmost part of Canada: Alaska (wholly), California, Connecticut, Idaho (wholly), Illinois, Indiana, Iowa, Maine (wholly), Massachusetts, Michigan, Minnesota (wholly), Montana (wholly), Nebraska, Nevada, New Hampshire (wholly), New York, North Dakota (wholly), Ohio, Oregon (wholly), Pennsylvania, Rhode Island, South Dakota (wholly), Utah, Vermont (wholly), Washington (wholly), Wisconsin (wholly), and Wyoming.

38. Branding cattle did not begin in the American West but in Connecticut, where a 1644 law required that all cattle and swine be earmarked or branded and that the marks should be registered.

39. The Sierra Nevada mountain range is in California.

40. The largest non-Alaskan national park in the United States is Death Valley National Park, which spans 3.4 million acres and is almost five times larger than its neighbor Yosemite. Hemmed in by nine mountains, Death Valley is a place of extremes, where a record high temperature of 134°F was recorded in 1913, and a ground temperature of 201°F has been recorded. It is also extreme in elevation: from 282 feet below sea level to 11,049 feet above, at the top of Telescope Peak. In short, Death Valley is the lowest, driest, and hottest location in the United States.

41. At eight thousand feet, Antarctica has the highest average elevation. The continent is about twice the size of Australia; its ice constitutes about 70 percent of the world's freshwater and 90 percent of the world's ice. Although 98 percent of Antarctica is ice, there is land beneath the ice, distinguishing the continent from the Arctic, which lies atop water. Antarctica's highest mountain, Vinson Massif, is more than sixteen thousand feet tall, higher than the highest peak in the Swiss Alps. With a mean temperature of 20°F below that of the Arctic, Antarctica is the coldest place on earth—a place where a temperature of –128°F was once recorded. (Lower temperatures, close to absolute zero, have been artificially created in labs.) Besides being the driest, coldest, and iciest continent, Antarctica is also the windiest continent, a place where there are often winds up to two hundred miles per hour.

42. The Netherlands is a country with twelve provinces, two of which (Noord-Holland, or North Holland, and Zuid-Holland, or South Holland) were created in 1840; Holland constitutes the northwestern portion of the Netherlands. Noord-Holland contains Amsterdam, the capital of the Netherlands, and Zuid-Holland contains

The Hague, the seat of government. *Netherlands*, by the way, means "low countries," and *Holland* means "wooded land." What we now call "the Netherlands" was called "the Napoleonic Kingdom of Holland" only between 1806 and 1810.

43. The Panama Canal does not receive ocean water; sitting about eighty-five feet above sea level, the water in the Panama Canal is freshwater, flowing from streams and lakes into Gatun Lake, which is formed by a dam on the Chagres River. The Atlantic and Pacific Oceans receive freshwater from the canal. A set of water-filled chambers, the Gatun Locks, lift ships entering from the Atlantic Ocean. The Pedro Miguel Locks and the Miraflores Locks lift ships entering from the Pacific Ocean.

44. The first skyscraper in America was the Home Insurance Building constructed in 1884 in Chicago, not New York City.

45. The largest lake in the world is the Caspian Sea. The largest enclosed body of water, the Caspian Sea has a surface area of more than 140,000 square miles. Bounded by southern Russia, western Kazakhstan and Turkmenistan, northern Iran, and eastern Azerbaijan, the Caspian Sea has a maximum depth of about 3,363 feet. By the way, the world's largest freshwater lake by surface area is Lake Superior, whereas Russia's Lake Baikal, the world's deepest lake, is the largest freshwater lake by volume, containing more water than all the North American Great Lakes combined but less than a third of the water in the Caspian Sea.

46. The largest sand desert is not the Sahara, which is largely rock, but the Great Arabian Desert (or Rub-al-Khali) in the Arabian peninsula.

47. The largest city park in the United States is not New York's Central Park, which is 843 acres, but Phoenix's South Mountain Park, which is about nineteen times larger than Central Park and features fifty-eight miles of trails for cycling, hiking, and horseback riding.

48. Most of the gold held in the United States is not at Fort Knox, Kentucky, but in the Federal Reserve vault at Wall Street in New York. Most of the gold there, however, does not belong to the United States but instead belongs to foreign accounts.

49. The Plains of Abraham are nowhere near Israel but are a historic 108-acre plateau within Battlefields Park in Quebec City, Canada; the landmark is named after Abraham Martin (1589–1664), a fisherman and river pilot who brought his animals to graze there.

50. The Battle of the Alamo was over the Republic of Texas, which included not only present-day Texas but also parts of New Mexico, Oklahoma, Kansas, and Wyoming.

Quiz 7
American History

1. Of what were George Washington's dentures made?

2. Who was the youngest president of the United States?

3. On what hill did the Battle of Bunker Hill occur?

4. Who led the Rough Riders up San Juan Hill in the Spanish-American War?

5. What was the name of the Confederate ironclad ship that fought the Union ironclad ship the *Monitor* on March 9, 1862?

6. Where was the American Civil War battle Shiloh fought?

7. What was George Armstrong Custer's rank during the Battle of Little Big Horn?

8. In which U.S. state can the oldest seat of Western government be found?

9. Who led the Indians in the battle of Little Bighorn?

10. What is the full title of the person who serves

as the Chief Justice of the United States Supreme Court?

11. What was the main reason the United States began gasoline rationing in 1942?

12. Until 1796, George Washington celebrated his birthday on what date?

13. Why was the Mason-Dixon line drawn?

14. What was Billy the Kid's real name?

15. Of the twenty-three nineteenth-century U.S. presidents, were there four, eight, or ten former military generals?

16. What was the longest war fought by the United States?

17. From President George Washington to President Barack Obama, how many individuals have been U.S. presidents?

18. What was the usual method of executing witches in Salem, Massachusetts?

19. Where were the first shots of the U.S. Civil War fired?

20. How much did Peter Minuit pay for Manhattan Island when he bought it from the Indians in 1626?

21. What was the verdict in the Lizzie Borden murder trial?

22. How many U.S. presidents have been impeached?

23. Between 1920 and 1933, what did American Prohibition prohibit?

24. Why did Ethan Allen (1738–1789) originally organize the Green Mountain Boys?

25. In the 1960s and 1970s, what did some feminists do with their bras?

26. Why was the Pentagon built with about twice as many bathrooms as would have been expected for a building of its size?

27. Most of the loss of life and property during the San Francisco earthquake of 1906 was due to what?

28. Why was Andrew Jackson called *Old Hickory*?

29. Roughly, how often did President Franklin D. Roosevelt deliver his famous fireside radio chats?

30. What was the name of the aviation sector of the U.S. Army during World War II?

31. Why did American colonists participate in the Boston Tea Party?

32. Who wrote George Washington's farewell address?

33. In 1837, the U.S. Postal Service adopted a seal showing a horse and rider. What, specifically, was the seal depicting?

34. Who was President Lincoln's first choice to command the Union army?

35. During Paul Revere's midnight ride through the Boston countryside on April 18, 1775, what warning did he shout?

36. What kind of hat did Daniel Boone wear?

37. What colors and styles of clothes did American Pilgrims wear?

38. How many U.S. states rejected the Prohibition Amendment (the 18th Amendment)?

39. When FDR ran against President Hoover, how did FDR criticize his opponent's handling of the Great Depression?

40. Which state describes itself as *Land of Opportunity*?

Quiz 7 Answers
American History

1. George Washington's false teeth were not made of wood but of hippopotamus and elephant ivory held together with gold springs. Real human teeth and bits of horse and donkey teeth were inserted into an ivory plate. By the way, his dentures are on display in the Smithsonian Institution's National Museum of History and Technology in Washington, DC.

2. The youngest person to become president of the United States was not John F. Kennedy, who was forty-three at the time of his inauguration in 1961, but Theodore Roosevelt, who was forty-two on the day he became president in 1901 after the assassination of President William McKinley. Although John F. Kennedy was the youngest person ever *elected* president, Theodore Roosevelt was the youngest person ever to hold the office.

3. The Battle of Bunker Hill was not fought at Bunker Hill, but at Breed's Hill, which was near Bunker Hill but steeper and closer to the British. What's more, Breed's Hill was then not in Boston but in Charlestown, Massachusetts, an independent town until Boston annexed it in 1874. William Prescott, famous for reportedly commanding his troops not to fire until they saw the whites of the enemy's eyes, defended Bunker Hill by fortifying Breed's Hill. Even though the British won the battle, they lost about one thousand men, boosting the colonists' morale. (By the way, Prescott might have mentioned the whites of the enemies' eyes, but some people ascribe the statement to Prescott's colleague General Israel ["Old Put"] Putnam. An 1849 history of the battle lists that statement as a command given in the battle but does not ascribe it to anyone in particular.)

4. The person who led the Rough Riders up San Juan Hill was not Theodore Roosevelt, who organized the First Regiment of the U.S. Cavalry Volunteers (the Rough Riders), but Colonel Leonard Wood who, on horseback, led the Rough Riders on foot in their charge up San Juan Hill, which was won on July 1, 1896. Lieutenant Colonel Theodore Roosevelt, Wood's second in command, had led the Rough Riders' charge up Kettle Hill earlier that day. The charge up Kettle Hill became mistaken for the Battle of San Juan Hill. The Rough Riders soon called themselves "Wood's Weary Walkers" because they fought much of the war on foot, not on horseback. The ships transporting the soldiers didn't have enough room for their horses, which had been left in Florida.

5. The Confederate ship was called the C.S.S. *Virginia* at the time of its battle with the *Monitor*, though it had been called the *Merrimack* earlier. The Confederates built the *Virginia* on what was left of the frigate U.S.S. *Merrimack* and gave the vessel a new name.

6. The Battle of Shiloh was not in Shiloh, Tennessee, but in Pittsburg Landing, Tennessee. The battle became known as Shiloh because of the presence of Shiloh Church near the center of the battlefield. The church was named for the original Shiloh, a biblical site north of Jerusalem destroyed by the Philistines about 1000 BCE.

7. George Armstrong Custer's rank during the Battle of Little Bighorn was not that of general, though he had been a brigadier general and had been promoted to a major general during the Civil War. After the war, Custer became a captain and was later promoted to lieutenant colonel (his actual rank when killed at the Little Bighorn).

8. The oldest seat of government in the United States can be found not in Massachusetts but in Santa Fe, New Mexico, whose governor's palace was built in 1610, ten years before the *Mayflower* landed in the New World.

9. The person who led the Indians in the Battle of Little Bighorn was not Sitting Bull, who stayed in the hills making medicine, but Crazy Horse.

10. The full title of the person who is the Chief Justice of the U.S. Supreme Court is not "Chief Justice of the Supreme Court" but "Chief Justice of the United States."

11. The main reason the U.S. government required gas rationing during World War II was not to save gas, since the Allies, at the beginning of the war, had control of about 85 percent of the world's oil production; rather, the United States instituted gasoline rationing to reduce tire use and conserve *rubber* until a synthetic product could be developed. Note that after Japan's incursion into Indochina, it controlled nearly all the world's natural rubber supply. It was estimated that the United States had only a one-year civilian supply of rubber in reserve, which was inadequate to meet the anticipated military demand for rubber during the war. The U.S. government wanted Americans to drive less, and rationing tires alone would not have accomplished that goal.

12. Until 1796, George Washington officially celebrated his birthday on February 11, not February 22. Because of the conversion from the Julian to the Gregorian calendar, George Washington was not born on Washington's birthday. Why was the Julian calendar replaced by the Gregorian calendar? By the sixteenth century, astronomers had observed a discrepancy between the existing Julian calendar, instituted in 46 BCE, and the true solar year. In 1582, Pope Gregory XIII implemented a revised calendar, which came to be known as the Gregorian, or New Style, Calendar and which required the elimination of ten days to correct the accumulated celestial error. The Gregorian Calendar included the present system of leap years to maintain accuracy. Numerous countries did not immediately adopt the new system. In fact, Britain and her colonies did not switch until 1752, by which time eleven days needed to be eliminated because of an even greater error in the Julian calendar. When the conversion took place in 1752, George Washington was twenty. Although he had been born on February 11, 1731 (Old Style), the date became February 22, 1732 (New Style), when colonial Virginia adopted the calendar and made the necessary adjustments.

13. The original purpose of the Mason-Dixon line was not to distinguish the North from the South during the U.S. Civil War but to settle a boundary in the eighteenth century between the Penn family of Pennsylvania and the Calvert family in Maryland. In 1760, the quarreling families agreed to have two English astronomers and surveyors, Charles Mason and Jeremiah Dixon, settle the dispute. From 1763 to 1767, Mason and Dixon established a boundary between latitude thirty-nine degrees, forty-three minutes, fifteen seconds and thirty-nine degrees, forty-three minutes, and twenty-three seconds. In reality, the east-west Mason-Dixon line is not a true line in a geometric sense but rather a series of adjoining lines.

14. Contrary to popular opinion, Billy the Kid's real name was not William H. Bonney (which was an alias he was using when he was sentenced to die), but probably Henry McCarty. Some accounts, however, contend that his original name was William Henry McCarty Jr., but his mother preferred to call him Henry and didn't want him known as Junior.

15. There were ten nineteenth-century American presidents who had been generals: Jackson, W. H. Harrison, Taylor, Pierce, A. Johnson, Grant, Hayes, Garfield, Arthur, and B. Harrison.

16. The longest war fought by the United States was the forty-six-year campaign against the Apache nation, which ended in 1886 with Geronimo's surrender in New Mexico.

17. There have been forty-three (not forty-four) men who have been president of the United States from Washington to Obama. President Grover Cleveland was president for two nonconsecutive terms, making him the twenty-second and twenty-fourth president.

18. Witches were executed in Salem, Massachusetts, not by being burned but by being hanged. During the Salem witch hunts, 14 women and 5 men were hanged, and 1 man (Giles Corey) was pressed to death under heavy stones. Although more than 150 others were imprisoned, and other women had been hanged as witches elsewhere in New England, witches weren't burned at the stake in Salem.

19. The first shots of the U.S. Civil War were not at Fort Sumter, South Carolina. South Carolina seceded from the Union and prepared to seize control of federal government forts in Charleston Harbor in 1860. On January 9, 1861, a battery of Confederate soldiers on Morris Island, South Carolina—cadets from the Citadel (military college)—fired seventeen shots at the *Star of the West*, a civilian Union steamship hired by the federal government to transport military supplies and reinforcements to the garrison of Fort Sumter. On April 12, 1861, three months later, the Confederate army fired on the South Carolina fort.

20. Although nearly everyone believes that Peter Minuit paid $24 for Manhattan, no money was exchanged. An unknown quantity of trinkets and goods was valued by the Dutch at 60 guilders, but, as said, no money was exchanged and dollars did not even exist until about 150 years later. So, then, how did we get the dollar estimate? In the 1840s, a New York newspaper writer speculated on the value of the American goods. Even though no record was made by the Dutch listing the specific items exchanged, the writer speculated that the goods given to the Indians 200 years earlier were worth $24.

21. Lizzie Borden's verdict was not guilty.

22. The number of U.S. presidents who have been impeached is two—namely, President Andrew Johnson and President Bill Clinton. Both were acquitted by the U.S. Senate; Johnson, by only one vote.

23. Prohibition in the United States (1920–1933) did not outlaw the possession or drinking of alcohol. Rather, the law made illegal "the manufacture, sale, or transportation of intoxicating liquors." The Eighteenth Amendment did not define *intoxicating liquor*, a task executed by the Volstead Act, which defined the term as "any drink at least 0.5 percent alcohol by volume." Note that it was quite legal for clubs, including the Yale Club, to serve alcoholic beverages bought before Prohibition. Note further that there were additional legal exemptions (some would say loopholes). For example, alcohol was available through a physician's prescription, and more people drank alcohol for medicinal purposes during Prohibition than before. Although writing prescriptions for alcohol during Prohibition served the financial interests of physicians, alcohol had been removed from the *Pharmacopeia of the United States* in 1916 and had been rejected as a tonic, stimulant, or food by the American Medical Association in 1917. Nonetheless, physicians were still able to prescribe liquor to patients on a specially designed governmental prescription form.

When the supply of medicinal whiskey was low, the government would increase its production, some of which would be diverted to bootleggers and corrupt individuals. Another exemption during Prohibition was sacramental wine. Many people certified themselves as ministers and rabbis to obtain and distribute large quantities of sacramental wine.

24. As an advocate of Vermont independence, Ethan Allen originally organized the Green Mountain Boys not to fight the British in the American Revolution but to fight off the Yorkers—that is, settlers from New York. Disputes arose because settlers from New York were given patents by the colonial governor of New Hampshire to land claimed by settlers from what was later Vermont, originally named New Hampshire Grants (1749–1777). Allen became involved in land speculation and was a proprietor in the New Hampshire Grants.

25. The feminists did not burn their bras but wore them. The closest thing to bra burning happened at the 1968 Miss America Pageant. On September 7, 1968, protesters of the pageant filled a "freedom trash can" with bras, girdles, false eyelashes, men's magazines, and other items they considered instruments of torture. Some people wanted to burn the items, but they were unable to obtain a permit. Journalist Lindsay van Gelder described the protest in an article for the *New York Post* whose headline was "Bra Burners and Miss America." That headline gave birth to an urban legend.

26. The Pentagon was built with about twice as many

bathrooms as would have been expected for a building of its size to comply with Virginia's then-legal code; Virginia law at the time required racial segregation of public buildings.

27. Most of the loss of life and property during the San Francisco earthquake of 1906 was due to the resultant fire, which raged for three days.

28. President Andrew Jackson was called *Old Hickory* because of his walking stick.

29. President Franklin Roosevelt did not deliver his chats weekly or monthly. In fact, on average, he gave one only two or three times a year (for a total of twenty-seven times between March 12, 1933, and his death in 1945).

30. The name of the aviation sector of the U.S. Army during World War II was not the "Army Air Force" or "Army Air Corps" but the "Army Air Forces" (note the plural), created on June 20, 1941, six months before Pearl Harbor. The Air Force, as a branch of the U.S. military, was created on July 26, 1947.

31. The colonists involved in the Boston Tea Party were *not* protesting against higher taxes on imported British tea. On the contrary, the price of tea had been lowered by the British. To understand the motives of those at the Boston Tea Party requires understanding a little history. Many goods imported into the colonies were heavily taxed by the British. To appease angry colonists, the British repealed the tariffs, except the tariff on tea, which the colonists circumvented by buying less-expensive, smuggled Dutch tea. The tea-buying preferences of the colonists led to millions of pounds of surplus British tea. To persuade the colonists to buy the surplus tea, the Parliament passed the Tea Act, which eliminated all duties on British tea and priced it below the cost of smuggled Dutch tea. Despite the lower cost of the British tea, many American colonists resented British involvement in what was increasingly regarded as an American (not British) economy. Accordingly, colonists refused to allow the unloading of the British tea. Then, on December 16, 1773, about sixty men dressed as Indians dumped the cargo of tea from the three British ships into Boston Harbor.

32. George Washington wrote his farewell address with the help of Alexander Hamilton.

33. The seal adopted in 1837 by the U.S. Postal Service was *not* depicting the Pony Express Service, which was a private service and which did not even begin until 1860; the original seal depicted an intercity postal rider. The Pony Express, by the way, went from St. Joseph, Missouri, to Sacramento, California, and lasted only a year and a half; it was made obsolete by the telegraph.

34. President Lincoln's first choice to lead the Union was not General Grant but Robert E. Lee, who rejected the offer because of his loyalty to Virginia.

35. Paul Revere did not shout, "The British are coming";

he shouted, "The regulars are out." The *regulars* were British infantry soldiers. Note, by the way, that many colonists still considered themselves British.

36. Contrary to the image of Daniel Boone popularized by actor Fess Parker on TV, the real Daniel Boone didn't wear a coonskin hat, which he thought looked uncivilized. Instead, he wore a beaver-felt hunter's hat, a wide-brimmed, Pennsylvania-style hat, which resembled the hat depicted on a box of Quaker oats. The coonskin hat became tied with Boone in the 1820s during a minstrel show called *The Hunters of Kentucky*, in which the actor portraying Boone was unable to find a beaver hat and wore a coonskin cap as the closest available substitute.

37. American Pilgrims didn't regularly dress in black, wear buckles, or black steeple hats. That image was formed in the nineteenth century when buckles suggested quaintness. Some male Pilgrims wore felt hats (but with no buckles), and female Pilgrims wore waistcoats that came in many colors. What's more, women's bodices or skirts were often blue, red, earth green, violet, or gray.

38. Although many people think that all the states ratified the Prohibition Amendment, two states (Rhode Island and Connecticut) rejected it.

39. FDR accused Hoover of overspending public money and ran on the promise that he would balance the budget and be more fiscally responsible than Hoover, who created public works programs. What's more, FDR's running mate in 1932, John Nance Garner, accused Hoover of moving the country toward socialism. Hoover, not FDR, was the first American president to systematically intervene in response to an economic downturn.

40. The state that describes itself as *Land of Opportunity* is Arkansas.

Quiz 8
Food

1. According to the Curtiss Candy Company, after whom was the Baby Ruth candy bar named?

2. After whom was the Caesar salad named?

3. After whom was German chocolate cake named?

4. After whom was the dish eggs Benedict named?

5. What is the source of the tails in oxtail soup?

6. What is headcheese?

7. What is the main purpose of searing meat?

8. What is sweetbread?

9. What distinguishes a hot dog from a frankfurter?

10. What is Welsh rabbit?

11. Why is telling Americans to serve red wine at room temperature possibly bad advice?

12. What is the most common main ingredient in mock turtle soup?

13. What percentage of buttermilk is butter?

14. Where were English muffins invented?

15. What country originated the hamburger?

16. What is the difference between mayonnaise and Miracle Whip?

17. What is the difference between Welsh rabbit and Welsh rarebit?

18. Why are some olives green rather than black?

19. What is the main difference between black tea and oolong tea?

20. What is the difference between cocoa and chocolate?

Quiz 8 Answers
Food

1. The Curtiss Candy Company insists that the Baby Ruth candy bar was named after Ruth Cleveland, the firstborn daughter of President Grover Cleveland. Note that the company never got legal permission from Babe Ruth to use what looks like a form of his name. According to Snopes.com, the candy bar was probably named after Babe Ruth, who had become enormously popular when the bar first came out—much more popular than Ruth Cleveland, who had died at the age of twelve, more than seventeen years before the candy bar was produced. Although the Curtiss Company has asserted that Ruth Cleveland had visited its factory, she could not have, since she had died before the factory was built.

2. The Caesar salad was named after Caesar Cardini, who created the Caesar salad in Mexico in 1924. The original recipe contained the same ingredients used today, minus the anchovies, which Cardini didn't think were needed with the tangy Worcestershire sauce.

3. German chocolate cake was named after Sam German, a man who in 1892 created a "sweet baking bar" named Baker's German's Sweet Chocolate. When the chocolate was used as an ingredient in recipes, apostrophes in its original name were left out, leading to the belief in German chocolate.

4. The dish called "eggs Benedict" was not named

after Benedict Arnold, the infamous traitor during the American Revolutionary War, but after socialite Samuel Benedict, who, when suffering from a hangover on a morning in 1894, ordered bacon and poached eggs on toast with Hollandaise sauce at New York's Waldorf-Astoria. Instead of receiving bacon and toast, Samuel Benedict received ham and an English muffin, which became a new breakfast sensation.

5. The tails in oxtail soup come not from oxen but from beef cattle.

6. Headcheese is not cheese but rather portions of the head, feet, and other parts of a pig pressed together and molded in the form of cheese.

7. The main purpose of searing meat is not to seal in moisture but to create a brown crust and to add flavor.

8. Sweetbread is not a bread but the thymus or pancreas of a young animal, usually a calf, though occasionally a lamb or pig.

9. A hot dog normally has a bun; a frankfurter need not have a bun.

10. Welsh rabbit is a cheese dish whose name is an ironic allusion to the poverty of those Welsh people who were too poor to afford meat.

11. Telling Americans to serve wine at room temperature may be bad advice because room temperature, in the wine-growing areas of Europe, is not the 70°F or 72°F

common in American homes. In much of Europe, room temperature is often 60°F to 65°F. Although drinking red wine between 55°F and 65°F is advisable, drinking it at 72°F will make it taste way out of balance. In short, it makes sense to serve red wine slightly chilled in much of the United States.

12. The most common main ingredient in mock turtle soup is a calf's head.

13. Buttermilk contains zero percent butter.

14. The English muffin was invented in America. In New York, about 1800, Samuel Bath Thomas, a baker who had emigrated from England, gave English muffins their name.

15. If by *hamburger*, one means the food that consists of a meat patty and a bun, the United States most likely originated it. Hamburg, Germany, however, originated a Hamburg steak (later called a *Hamburger steak*) during the latter part of the nineteenth century. The meat originally had no bun.

16. Mayonnaise is a dressing that consists of raw egg yolks, oil, lemon juice or vinegar, and spices; Miracle Whip, which debuted at the 1933 Chicago World's Fair, consists of mayonnaise blended with cheaper dressings, more than twenty spices, high-fructose corn syrup, and sugar.

17. Welsh rabbit, as indicated in question 10, is no more a species of rabbit than a decoy duck is a species of duck; the expression *Welsh rabbit* became mangled by some people into *Welsh rarebit*, which describes the same thing, to wit, melted cheese on toast.

18. Green olives, unlike black olives, have been picked before they're ripe.

19. Black tea leaves have been completely fermented before being dried; oolong tea leaves have been only partly fermented before being dried.

20. Both cocoa and chocolate are derived from the seeds of a tropical tree called *Theobroma cacao*. After the seeds or beans are roasted, shelled, and ground, they cool in pans, producing, at first, a paste and then solid bars, consisting partly of a fat called cocoa butter. The combination of cocoa butter and cocoa is what we call chocolate. If the paste is put into pressured containers, the fat separates from the mixture, producing cocoa.

Quiz 9
Science

1. From what metal is tin foil made?

2. In what part of your body does most digestion occur?

3. What is petrified wood?

4. What shape is a raindrop?

5. What shape is the Earth?

6. What causes tidal waves?

7. What, if anything, distinguishes a cranium from a skull?

8. What are icebergs?

9. If you threw dry ice (solid carbon dioxide) into a fire, what would happen?

10. Which metal or metals are liquid at room temperature?

11. What makes champagne fizz?

12. What element is the best conductor of heat and electricity?

13. In producing echoes, is there anything unique about a duck's quack?

14. What is true about pet fur and allergies?

15. What is one hearing when one places a seashell next to an ear?

16. Is it possible to swallow food while standing on one's head?

17. Ecologically speaking, which is worse (all things considered) for the environment, paper or plastic bags?

18. What is the red liquid that oozes out of a very rare steak?

19. When is mammal blood blue?

20. What is true about the human tongue's ability to detect different tastes in its different regions?

Quiz 9 Answers
Science

1. Tin foil is made not from tin but from aluminum.

2. Most digestion occurs not in the stomach, which stores food and reduces it to a pulpy mass, but in the small intestine.

3. Petrified wood is not wood that has become stone but wood in which mineral water fills cells, replacing the original fibers until the whole log structure has become solid stone. In other words, petrified wood isn't wood but stone, even though it shows the details of the original wood.

4. A raindrop is not teardrop shaped but spherical.

5. The shape of the Earth is not that of an ordinary sphere; rather, the Earth is an oblate spheroid, meaning that it bulges at the equator and is flattened at the poles, making the length of the equator slightly greater than the distance around via the North Pole and the South Pole.

6. Tidal waves are caused not by tides but by underwater disturbances, such as earthquakes, landslides, or volcanic activity. To avoid confusion, many scientists prefer the word *tsunami* to the word *tidal wave*.

7. The cranium is the part of the skull enclosing the brain, consisting of all the bones of the skull except one, the inferior maxillary, or mandible (the lower jaw).

8. Icebergs are not frozen ocean water but masses of ice broken off from glaciers or ice sheets, formed from snow that has been compressed into ice by its own weight over thousands of years.

9. Dry ice thrown into a fire wouldn't melt but would sublime, meaning that it would change directly into a gas.

10. Although many people know that mercury (the stuff in some thermometers) is liquid at room temperature, fewer people know that the metals gallium (Ga), caesium (Cs), and francium (Fr) can also be liquids at or near room temperature.

11. Champagne fizzes not because of carbon dioxide but because of dirt, dust, or lint. Because carbon dioxide molecules would evaporate invisibly in a completely smooth, clean glass, scientists used to think that the slight imperfections in the glass enabled bubbles to form. New photographic evidence, however, reveals that the nicks and grooves in a glass are too small for bubbles to latch on to. Instead, it is the microscopic particles of dust in the glass that enable bubbles to form. The dirt or dust in the glass acts as condensation nuclei for the dissolved carbon dioxide.

12. Although many people think that copper is the best conductor of heat and electricity, silver actually is. Copper, the second most conductive element, is used in electrical equipment because it is much cheaper than silver.

13. Contrary to a popular misconception, a duck's

quack will produce an echo, though it may be difficult for us to hear it in some circumstances.

14. Normally, people who have allergic reactions around pets aren't allergic to fur but to pet dander (dead skin flakes), saliva, or urine/droppings. Regularly washing pets can often reduce allergic reactions.

15. The sound that appears to be originating from inside the shell is the sound of our own blood rushing through veins in the ear, coupled with the echoes of nearby sounds. Any cup-shaped object can produce the effect.

16. It is possible to swallow food while standing on one's head. Contrary to popular belief, food does not simply fall down the esophagus as a person swallows, but food is gradually pulled down the ten-inch passage to the stomach. Swallowing is a complex act in which food moves from the mouth to the stomach. The process does not work simply by gravity but involves constrictive and peristaltic waves that move food down the esophagus in rhythmic muscular contractions. Gravity can, though, speed up the process, as can be seen when liquids are swallowed more rapidly than solids.

17. Although both plastic bags and paper bags are environmentally inferior to reusable canvas bags, plastic bags, all things considered, are better than paper bags. For example, the manufacturing process to produce paper bags requires much more energy than that required for producing plastic bags. What's more, manufacturing paper bags produces more greenhouse gases, acid rain, and water pollutants than are produced by manufacturing plastic bags. Still further, recycling paper bags requires much more energy than that required for recycling plastic bags. Moreover, paper bags take up more space than plastic bags in a landfill. True, paper bags degrade much faster than plastic ones, and plastic bags can threaten wildlife. Nonetheless, there are more environmental negatives associated with paper bags than with plastic ones.

18. The red liquid that oozes out of a very rare steak isn't blood, but myoglobin, a relative of blood. Myoglobin is a single-chain globular protein that is structurally related to hemoglobin. Hemoglobin conveys oxygen through the body by the bloodstream. Because many animals need oxygen in the muscles faster than the circulatory system can deliver it, they store myoglobin in their muscles. If an animal is running away from a predator, the muscles use the myoglobin while hemoglobin is en route. Almost all the blood in a very rare steak has already been removed before the steak is delivered to the market.

19. Mammal blood is not ever blue but is bright red or scarlet (when it is oxygenated) or a darker red (when it is not oxygenated). True, veins make blood appear blue through the skin but that appearance is due to a phenomenon known as Rayleigh scattering, the same effect that is responsible for apparently blue skies. Rayleigh scattering, named after the English physicist Lord Rayleigh, is the elastic scattering of light or other electromagnetic radiation by particles much smaller than the wavelength of light.

20. Different tastes can be detected by taste buds on all parts of the tongue. The belief in a "tongue map" stems from a mistranslation by a Harvard psychologist of a discredited German paper written in 1901. Yes, we may have increased sensitivity to certain qualities in certain areas of our tongues, but we perceive all taste qualities all over our tongues.

Literature

1. In Mary Shelley's 1818 novel *Frankenstein, or the Modern Prometheus*, what was the name of the monster?

2. Within 20 percent, what percentage of the protagonists in Horatio Alger's rags-to-riches novels become millionaires?

3. In Longfellow's words "the village smithy stands," what does *smithy* describe?

4. Tennyson wrote in the poem "In Memoriam" the following words: "'Tis better to have loved and lost / than never to have love at all." What sort of love was he describing?

5. "This world is a comedy to those who think, a tragedy to those who feel." Who wrote those words?

6. Who was Phineas Fogg?

7. Who was the first person to say or write "Ignorance is bliss"?

8. Who was the first to say or write "Alas! Poor Yorick. I knew him well"?

9. The word *wherefore* in "Wherefore art thou, Romeo?" means what?

10. In L. Frank Baum's book *The Wonderful Wizard of Oz*, what were Dorothy's shoes made of?

11. According to Ian Fleming's novels and short stories, which alcoholic beverage does James Bond consume most often?

12. What is the color of the original Oompa-Loompas in Roald Dahl's 1964 children's novel *Charlie and the Chocolate Factory*?

13. The 1865 story "Hans Brinker, or the Silver Skates" relates how a fifteen-year-old Dutch boy, Hans Brinker, saves his town by plugging a leaky dike with his finger. In what country did the story originate?

14. What was the official name for the schoolbook popularly known as *McGuffey's Reader*?

15. What was the original title of Dante Alighieri's *Divine Comedy* (1320)?

16. What sort of hat did Sherlock Holmes wear?

17. Who wrote *Grimm's Fairy Tales*?

18. To whom did F. Scott Fitzgerald address the remark that the rich are very different from you and me?

19. During his lifetime, what was Noah Webster's bestselling book?

20. Where did Abraham Lincoln write the Gettysburg Address?

Quiz 10 Answers
Literature

1. The name of the monster in Mary Shelley's 1818 novel was not "Frankenstein" (which was the name of the monster's creator, Victor Frankenstein) but "Adam," which is also the traditional name of the first man.

2. Zero percent of Horatio Alger's protagonists became millionaires, though many of them became financially respectable.

3. *Smithy* does not designate a blacksmith but a blacksmith's shop. In fact, in the same poem, Longfellow writes, "The smith a mighty man is he," making it clear that the *smithy* is the shop, and the *smith* is the blacksmith.

4. Tennyson was not describing a romantic heterosexual love. Tennyson was describing the profoundly deep friendship he had with Arthur Hallam, who had died at twenty-two. Tennyson met Hallam at Cambridge University and found in Hallam a kind of father figure he might have missed at home. His father took up the ministry because he had been disinherited and ended up a drunkard. One of Tennyson's brothers was a drug addict, and another spent his life in a mental hospital. Queen Victoria was so impressed by "In Memoriam" that Tennyson was appointed poet laureate.

5. Contrary to popular opinion, the author of "This

world is a comedy to those who think, a tragedy to those who feel" was not George Bernard Shaw (1856–1950) but Horace Walpole (1717–1797).

6. Phineas Fogg is probably someone mistaken for the hero of Jules Verne's *Around the World in Eighty Days*, whose name is *Phileas Fogg*.

7. The first person to say "Ignorance is bliss" was probably the first person to misquote the poet Thomas Gray, who, in "Ode on a Distant Prospect of Eton College," wrote, "where ignorance is bliss, 'Tis folly to be wise."

8. The first person to say or write "Alas! Poor Yorick. I knew him well" was probably the first person to misquote Hamlet, who said: "Alas! Poor Yorick! I knew him, Horatio."

9. *Wherefore* does not mean "where" but "why." The famous line from *Romeo and Juliet* is spoken by Juliet during the balcony scene. She is lamenting the antagonism between her family (the Capulets) and Romeo's family (the Montagues). Juliet is asking, "Romeo, why did you have to be a Montague?"

10. In the book *The Wonderful Wizard of Oz*, Dorothy's shoes were not made of rubies, as in the movie, but made of silver. Noel Langley, a Hollywood screenwriter, changed them to rubies for the film *The Wizard of Oz*. By the way, the book doesn't contain Miss Gulch, the farmhands, or Professor Marvel in Kansas. In fact, Dorothy actually goes to Oz and doesn't meet the Wicked Witch until she gets to the witch's castle.

11. According to Ian Fleming's writings (as revealed at AtomicMartinis.com), James Bond's favorite alcoholic beverage isn't a vodka martini (shaken not stirred) but bourbon. Of the 317 drinks consumed, Bond drank 37 bourbons, 10 bourbon and branch waters, and 7 bourbon and sodas, but only 19 vodka martinis.

12. The original Oompa-Loompas were black, not orange. In the first edition of the novel *Charlie and the Chocolate Factory*, the Oompa-Loompas were a tribe of black pygmies imported by Mr. Wonka from "the very deepest and darkest part of the African jungle where no white man had been before," to replace the white workers who were let go. The Oompa-Loompas came to live on chocolate but originally ate "beetles, eucalyptus leaves, caterpillars, and the bark of the bong-bong tree." In the early 1970s, Roald Dahl's U.S. publisher, Knopf, insisted that the Oompa-Loompas be redescribed because their original description appeared to have overtones of slavery and seemed close to racism. In 1972, there appeared a revised edition of *Charlie and the Chocolate Factory*, in which the Oompa-Loompas were not black pygmies but were closer to little hippies with "golden-brown hair" and "rosy-white skin." Later, they were depicted as futuristic punks with Mohawk haircuts. In the 1971 movie *Willy Wonka and the Chocolate Factory*, the Oompa-Loompas appear as orange elves. The 2005 movie has a different title and the Oompa-Loompas in it aren't unambiguously orange.

13. *Hans Brinker, or the Silver Skates*, written by Mary Mapes Dodge, originated in the United States. The story did, however, spread to the Netherlands, where there is a statue honoring the fictitious hero.

14. The official name of the schoolbook popularly known as *McGuffey's Reader* was *McGuffey's Eclectic Reader*.

15. The original title of the *Divine Comedy* was just *Comedy* (*Commedia*) in Italian. Later, the author and poet Giovanni Boccaccio added the word *divine* (*divina*).

16. Although the deerstalker hat is almost a trademark of Sherlock Holmes, he never wore one. Nowhere in Sir Arthur Conan Doyle's four novels and fifty-six stories is the hat mentioned. In fact, the deerstalker, appropriate for rural people (especially hunters), would not suit the fashion-conscious urbanite Sherlock Holmes. Designed by the detective himself, Holmes's hat is not a traditional deerstalker. The mistaken belief that Holmes wore such a hat can be traced to Sidney Paget, the illustrator of *Strand Magazine*. Paget, who liked deerstalkers and would at times wear them, produced drawings—inaccurately—depicting Holmes wearing the hat.

17. The inventors of *Grimm's Fairy Tales* were not Jacob and Wilhelm Grimm. The Grimm's brothers simply compiled traditional fairy tales from previously published collections and recorded folklore told by peasant storytellers.

18. The words about the rich were not in an actual conversation between F. Scott Fitzgerald and Ernest Hemingway or between any two actual persons; rather, the words are from the unnamed narrator of Fitzgerald's short story "The Rich Boy." Many people think that Fitzgerald and Hemingway were talking about the rich in a conversation in which Fitzgerald first asserts that the very rich are different from you (Hemingway) and me (Fitzgerald), and then Hemingway replies, "Yes, they have more money." Instead, Fitzgerald's words about the very rich appear in "The Rich Boy," in the third paragraph:

> Let me tell you about the very rich. They are different from you and me. They possess and enjoy early, and it does something to them, makes them soft where we are hard, and cynical, where we are trustful, in a way that, unless you were born rich, it is very difficult to understand.

The words, then, are not addressed to Hemingway but to the readers of the story. Hemingway, however, connected himself to "The Rich Boy" in August 1936, ten years after Fitzgerald's story was published in *Redbook* magazine. In Hemingway's short story "The Snows of Kilimanjaro," the narrator is a dying writer named Harry, who is presented as remembering "poor Scott Fitzgerald" and "his romantic awe" of the rich. Harry remembers that "someone" had said of the rich, "Yes, they have more money." Note that Fitzgerald's statement about the rich and Hemingway's reply are fictional and appear in two different short stories published a decade apart. Again, and contrary to popular belief, the remarks were not part of an actual conversation between the two authors. After "The Snows of Kilimanjaro" came out, Fitzgerald wrote Hemingway an angry and sad letter, asking the author not to mention him again in his fiction. In reprints of Hemingway's story, the character Scott Fitzgerald became Julian.

19. Noah Webster's bestselling book during his lifetime was not his dictionary but a spelling book, *The Blue-Backed Speller*, which was published in 1783 and which, by 1800, had sold more than a million copies.

20. Contrary to popular belief, Abraham Lincoln did not write the Gettysburg Address on the back of an envelope while riding a train to Gettysburg. In fact, he began the first draft for the speech on November 8, 1862, eleven days before the event. Indeed, there were five drafts of the speech, each on White House stationery. Further, the Associated Press had been given an advance copy of the speech so that they could print it in the newspapers.

Astronomy

1. What object created by people can be seen from the moon?

2. Which country landed the first craft on the moon?

3. What planet in our solar system has the hottest mean surface temperature?

4. Which is farther from the sun, Neptune or Pluto?

5. What is the brightest star in the night sky of the Northern Hemisphere?

6. What causes Earth's seasons?

7. Although a few moons of Uranus are named after characters in Alexander Pope's "The Rape of the Lock," most are named after what?

8. What is the English adjective to describe the planet Jupiter?

9. What is the English adjective now generally used to describe the planet Venus and its hypothetical inhabitants?

10. Who was the first person to assert that Earth orbits around the sun?

11. What is true about the landing temperature of most meteorites?

12. What is the difference between the Evening Star and the Morning Star?

Quiz 11 Answers
Astronomy

1. No humanly created object, including the Great Wall of China, can be seen from the moon, more than 200,000 miles from Earth. In 1969, astronaut Alan Bean, who walked on the moon during the *Apollo 12* mission, wrote that all he could see when looking at Earth was a beautiful sphere, which was mostly white (clouds), some blue (oceans), patches of yellow (deserts), and spots of green (vegetation).

2. The country that first landed a craft on the moon was not the United States of America, which can boast all twelve moon walkers, but the former Soviet Union, whose *Luna 2* became in 1959 the first unmanned space probe to crash-land on the moon. In February 1966, after soft-landing *Luna 9* on the moon, the former Soviet Union relayed the first pictures directly from the lunar surface. In June 1966, the America's *Surveyor I* became the first U.S. spacecraft to soft-land on the moon. In July 1969, the United States landed the first human being on the moon, Neil Armstrong.

3. The planet in our solar system with the highest mean surface temperature is not Mercury (the closest to the sun) but Venus (whose gases, mostly carbon dioxide, trap the heat).

4. Pluto is usually farther from the sun than Neptune is, but not always; Pluto's highly eccentric (elliptical) orbit shows that a small region of Pluto's orbit lies closer to the sun than Neptune's orbit. For example, Pluto was interior to Neptune's orbit between February 7, 1979, and February 11, 1999. The last period in which Pluto was in that portion of its orbit lasted only fourteen years, from July 11, 1935, to September 15, 1949.

5. The brightest star in the night sky of the Northern Hemisphere is not the North Star (Polaris) but Sirius (the Dog Star).

6. Earth's seasons are determined not by its distance from the sun but by its tilted axis. In July, when it is summer in the Northern Hemisphere, Earth is farthest from the sun, but the northern part of the planet is tilted toward the sun, giving longer days and more direct sunlight. In winter, Earth is tilted away. The seasons are reversed in the Southern Hemisphere, which is tilted toward the sun in January and away from it in July.

7. Most of Uranus's moons are named after Shakespearean characters. Uranus has more than two dozen moons, including Titania, Oberon, and Puck (all from *A Midsummer Night's Dream*); Cordelia (from *King Lear*); Ophelia (from *Hamlet*); Portia (from *The Merchant of Venice*); and Rosalind (from *As You Like It*).

8. The English adjective for the planet Jupiter is *Jovian*.

9. The English adjective now generally used to describe the planet Venus and its hypothetical inhabitants is not *Venusian* but *Cytherean*, from *Cytheria*, a small island now part of Greece where Aphrodite emerged on a seashell. By the way, the expression *venereal disease* pays homage to Venus, the Roman goddess of love.

10. The first person to assert that Earth revolves around the sun was not Copernicus (1473–1543), but some unnamed ancient thinkers. The heliocentric theory appeared in Sanskrit texts dating from the seventh century BCE. Further, some ancient Greeks theorized about it in the third and fourth centuries BCE. What's more, an Arab astronomer suggested the heliocentric theory in the fourteenth century, a hundred years before Copernicus was born. Copernicus became famous not only because of his assertion of the heliocentric theory but also because of his mathematical calculations offered as proof of the theory.

11. Most meteorites are not hot upon landing. In fact, many have frost on them. A meteor's speed during atmospheric reentry is enough to melt or vaporize its outermost layer, quickly blowing off any molten material. The interior of the meteor does not have time to heat up because rocks are poor conductors of heat. What is more, atmospheric drag can slow down earthbound meteors, giving their surface time to cool down.

12. Both the *Evening Star* and the *Morning Star* refer to the planet Venus, depending on which time of day it is dominating the darkness. Throughout the fall and winter of 2008–2009, Venus was the most notable object in the evening sky in the west to southwest.

Quiz 12
Names (Part I)

1. How did mobile homes get their name?

2. After what animals were the Canary Islands named?

3. At Stanford University, the term *Stanford cardinal* refers to what?

4. Why are bloodhounds called bloodhounds?

5. How did the bird called the Baltimore oriole get its name?

6. How did the American bald eagle get its name?

7. What was the complete name used by Mr. Cooper, the man who hijacked a Boeing 727 in 1977 and who took $200,000?

8. Why are hangnails so named?

9. What is the official name of the world's largest train station, which is at 42nd Street and Park Avenue in Midtown Manhattan in New York?

10. What are the residents of Lawrence, Kansas, called?

11. What are the residents of Leavenworth, Kansas, called? Spell the name.

12. What was President Coolidge's first name?

13. What was President Wilson's first name?

14. What are the residents of Norfolk, England, called?

15. What are the residents of Norfolk, Nebraska, called?

16. What are the residents of Norfolk, Virginia, called?

17. What are the residents of Phoenix, Arizona, called?

18. What are the residents of Charlestown, Massachusetts, called?

19. What are the residents of Oxford, England, called?

20. What are the residents of Cambridge, England, called?

21. What are the residents of Moscow, Idaho, called?

22. What are the residents of New Orleans, Louisiana, called?

23. What is the official name of the U.S. Chamber of Commerce?

24. What are the residents of Richmond, California, called?

25. What are the residents of Richmond, Virginia, called?

Quiz 12 Answers
Names (Part I)

1. Mobile homes did not get their name from their mobility but from Mobile, Alabama, the city where the houses first boomed. Invented by James and Laura Sweet to solve housing problems after World War II, mobile homes were originally known as Sweet homes. During the 1950s, many firms set up in Mobile, Alabama, to take advantage of cheap labor. Mobile homes were mass-produced, and the name stuck. (Note, however, that the name of the Alabama city is pronounced *moh-BEEL*.)

2. The Canary Islands were not named after canary birds but after dogs. Located in the Atlantic Ocean off northwest Africa, the Canary Islands were named for the extinct race of large dogs (Latin *Canis*) that once roamed the island. It is believed that the Roman scholar Pliny the Elder, who called one of the islands "Canaria," was responsible for their names. In any event, the canary bird is so named because it comes from the Canary Islands; the islands did not acquire their name from the canary bird.

3. The term *Stanford cardinal* refers not to a bird but to the school color of Stanford University.

4. Bloodhounds are so named not because of any special ability to smell blood but because they were the first breed of dog whose blood, or breeding, records were maintained.

5. The name of the bird called the *Baltimore oriole* does not come from the city of Baltimore, which was settled decades after the bird acquired its name; instead, the bird derived its name from the adopted name of the founder of Maryland in 1632, George Calvert, who assumed the title of Lord Baltimore and took black and orange as the family's colors. The Baltimore oriole derived its name because its colors matched those of the Baltimore family. Although the city was founded in 1729, the bird had already been known as the Baltimore bird by 1669.

6. The American bald eagle does not get its name from being bald, which it is not; rather, the eagle's name was originally the *balded* eagle, referring to the Middle English word *balded* ("white" or "having white fur or feathers"). The eagle has slicked-down white feathers covering its head.

7. Cooper never referred to himself as "D. B. Cooper" but as "Dan Cooper."

8. Hangnails are so named not because anything about them hangs but because they hurt; *ang* in Old English meant "pain."

9. The official name of the world's largest train station is not *Grand Central Station*, which is the name of the nearby post office as well as the name of a previous station on the site and the name of a Manhattan subway station at the same location. The technically correct term for the world's largest train station is *Grand Central Terminal*.

10. The residents of Lawrence, Kansas, are Lawrentians, as distinguished from Lawrencians, who are residents of Lawrence, Massachusetts.

11. The residents of Leavenworth, Kansas, are Leavenwortheans.

12. President Coolidge's first name was not Calvin but John; he was John Calvin Coolidge.

13. President Woodrow Wilson's first name was not Woodrow but Thomas; he was Thomas Woodrow Wilson.

14. The residents of Norfolk, England, are North Anglians.

15. The residents of Norfolk, Nebraska, are Norfolkans.

16. The residents of Norfolk, Virginia, are Norfolkians.

17. The residents of Phoenix, Arizona, are Phoenicians.

18. The residents of Charlestown, Massachusetts, are Townies.

19. The residents of Oxford, England, are Oxonians, as are graduates of Oxford University.

20. The residents of Cambridge, England, and Cambridge, Massachusetts, and graduates of Cambridge University are all Cantabrigians.

21. The residents of Moscow, Idaho, are Moscowites.

22. The residents of New Orleans are Orleanians.

23. The official name of the U.S. Chamber of Commerce is the Chamber of Commerce of the United States of America.

24. The residents of Richmond, California, are Richmondites.

25. The residents of Richmond, Virginia, are Richmonders.

Names (Part II)

1. What are the residents of Rochester, New York, called?

2. What are the residents of Rochester, Indiana, called?

3. How did the software company Adobe get its name?

4. How did Xerox get its name?

5. What are the residents of Arkansas City, Arkansas, called?

6. What was the official name of the bed created by the Murphy Door Bed Company?

7. What is the official name of what we call the Congressional Medal of Honor?

8. How did bulldogs acquire their name?

9. What was Hitler's original last name?

10. What is the king of the jungle?

11. What did the famous Hollywood sign on a hill originally say?

12. Why is the name Fido associated with dogs?

13. What is the difference between an Egyptian sphinx and a Greek sphinx?

14. How did San Francisco's Golden Gate Bridge get its name?

15. How did the quarter horse get its name?

16. How did the monkey wrench get its name?

17. How did Wall Street get its name?

18. After whom was Pennsylvania named?

19. How did the world's tallest waterfall, Angel Falls, which is in Venezuela, get its name?

20. How did Russia's Red Square get its name?

21. What are the residents of Derbyshire, England, called?

22. What are the residents of Exeter, England, called?

23. What are the residents of Plains, Georgia (home of President Carter), called?

24. What are the residents of Punxsutawney, Pennsylvania, called?

25. What are the residents of Shropshire, England, called?

Quiz 13 Answers
Names (Part II)

1. The residents of Rochester, New York, are called Rochesterians.

2. The residents of Rochester, Indiana, are called Rochesterites.

3. The software company Adobe gets its name from the Adobe Creek, which ran behind the home of the company's founder, John Warnock.

4. The name *Xerox* comes from its connection to dry copies. Unlike a mimeograph, which made wet copies, Xerox used xerography, the name of which comes from the Greek word for "dry" (*xeros*).

5. The residents of Arkansas City, Arkansas, are Arkansas Citians.

6. The official name of the bed created by the Murphy Door Bed Company was not *Murphy bed* but *In-a-Door*.

7. The official name of what we call the Congressional Medal of Honor is *Medal of Honor*, though it is presented "in the name of the Congress of the United States."

8. Bulldogs acquired their name not because of their appearance but because of their use in the sport of bull-baiting in medieval England. The dogs were trained to fasten on a bull's snout and hang on.

9. Hiedler was Adolf Hitler's original last name, not Schicklgruber. Adolf Hitler's father, Alois, was born to an unmarried woman named Anna Schicklgruber. When Alois was five years old, his mother married a miller named Johann George Hiedler, who signed papers saying that he was Alois's father. Until his mid-thirties, Alois went by his mother's maiden name and then decided to change his name to Hiedler, which he spelled *Hitler*. Alois's third wife, Klara Pölzl, bore him three children. The third child was named Adolf Hitler at birth. Hitler's enemies learned about Anna Schicklgruber and called him Schicklgruber as an insult.

10. Strictly speaking, there is no universally accepted king of the jungle. The lion is often considered the king of the jungle, but the king of the jungle cannot literally be the lion, which does not even live in the jungle but on the plains, where lionesses (not lions) usually hunt and kill. The males usually protect the den. Note further that, unlike lions, healthy, full-grown elephants have no natural enemies but human beings. Because male lions are "crowned," "rule" the pride, and look majestic, it is understandable why people would call them kings.

11. The famous Hollywood sign originally said "Hollywoodland." The sign was built in 1928 as an oversize novelty ad for Hollywood Realty. The "land" part fell off and was never replaced.

12. *Fido* is associated with dogs because dogs are associated with loyalty, and *Fido* is from the Latin word *fidus* ("faithful" or "loyal").

13. An Egyptian sphinx was commonly presented as having a man's head (usually that of a pharaoh but sometimes that of a ram or a hawk) and a lion's body in a recumbent position; a Greek sphinx, in contrast, was a mythological creature having the head and chest of a woman, the body of a lion, and wings. Often depicted in a seated position, a Greek sphinx would be no larger than an average lion.

14. The Golden Gate Bridge was not named after the Gold Rush. In fact, the bridge received its name two years before James W. Marshall discovered gold at John Sutter's mill in the Sacramento Valley. Instead, the name of the bridge comes from explorer John C. Frémont, who named it after the Golden Horn, the inlet forming the harbor for Istanbul, Turkey, because the entrance to San Francisco reminded him of that harbor. By the way, Frémont became the first Republican nominee for the president of the United States.

15. The quarter horse acquired its name because it ran in quarter-mile races.

16. The monkey wrench was named after its inventor, Charles Moncky.

17. Wall Street got its name not from the tall buildings, which seem to wall it in, but a wall that used to be across Manhattan Island to keep out the Indians.

18. Pennsylvania was not named after Pennsylvania's founder, William Penn (1644–1718), but after his father, Sir William Penn (1621–1670), who lent Charles II £16,000 and whose son asked that the debt be repaid with land north of Maryland.

19. Angel Falls gets its name not from association with angels but from American aviator Jimmie Angel, who flew over them on November 16, 1933, as he was searching for a valuable ore bed. Angel Falls had been sighted before; Venezuelan explorer Ernesto Sanchez La Cruz is said to have spotted the falls in 1912, though he did not publicize the discovery of them at the time.

20. Moscow's Red Square did not get its name from Communist associations. Note that the name "Red Square" unlike Russian communism, has existed since the 1600s. Its Russian name includes the word *krasnaya*, translatable as either "beautiful" or "red" (though it originally meant "beautiful"), describing nearby Saint Basil's Cathedral, which was commissioned by Ivan the Terrible. Reportedly, Ivan blinded the architect responsible for the cathedral to ensure that he would never design anything equally beautiful.

21. The residents of Derbyshire, England, are Darybites or Darbians.

22. The residents of Exeter, England, are Exonians. The term *Exonian* is also used for students and graduates of schools with "Exeter" in their names, such as Phillips Exeter Academy in Exeter, New Hampshire.

23. The male residents of Plains, Georgia, are Plainsmen; the female residents are Plainswomen.

24. The residents of Punxsutawney, Pennsylvania, are Punxyites.

25. The residents of Shropshire, England, are Salopians, from *Salop*, another name for "Shropshire."

Time

1. The Oktoberfest beer festival begins in what month?

2. In what month is Cambridge University's May Bumps boat race held?

3. If it's noon in Pensacola, Florida, what time is it in Fargo, North Dakota?

4. When was the first day of the current century?

5. How often does a leap year occur?

6. In what decade was the car called the Stutz Bearcat introduced?

7. If it is noon on a Tuesday at the South Pole, what time is it at the North Pole?

8. When is the summer solstice in the Northern Hemisphere?

9. If it's noon in California, what time is it in Kentucky?

10. Which has more time zones, the People's Republic of China or Alaska?

Quiz 14 Answers
Time

1. The Oktoberfest beer festival begins in September, though it originally began in October.

2. The Cambridge University's May Bumps boat race begins in June, though it used to be celebrated in May.

3. If it is noon in Pensacola, Florida, it is noon in Fargo, North Dakota, because they are both in the Central Time Zone.

4. The first day of the current century was January 1, 2001. Because there is no zero in the Christian era calendar, and the first century lasted from year AD 1 (or 1 CE) to the end of the year 100, the second century began in the year 101, and the twenty-first century began in the year 2001.

5. A leap year is not *every* year divisible by four because years divisible by one hundred but not by four hundred are *not* leap years. For example, 1800 and 1900 are years divisible by four but are not leap years. In contrast, the year 2000 was a leap year. Why are there exceptions? According to our calendar (the Gregorian calendar), the year has 365¼ days. To make up for the quarter day lost because the calendar has room for only 365 days, the day is traditionally added every four years and traditionally after February 28, giving us February 29. In reality, however, the year isn't exactly 365¼ days but 365¼ days and a few extra minutes. To make things come out right, exceptions were made to the rule about leap years, making them usually, but not always, occur every four years.

6. The Stutz Bearcat was introduced in the second decade of the twentieth century (1914), though it is associated with the 1920s.

7. The question asking for the time on the North Pole is unanswerable because there are no universally accepted criteria for time on the North Pole, though the question would be answerable for the South Pole, whose time has been coordinated with that of New Zealand. People at the North Pole may choose whichever time zone is convenient, such as Greenwich Mean Time or the time zone of the country from which they departed.

8. The summer solstice is usually on June 21 in the Northern Hemisphere, but it can also fall on June 22 in years preceding leap years. Likewise, the winter solstice in the Northern Hemisphere is usually on December 21, but it can also fall on December 22 in years preceding leap years.

9. If it's noon in California, it is both 2 p.m. and 3 p.m. in Kentucky because Kentucky is one of the thirteen U.S. states divided into two time zones. Although any one place in Kentucky will have one time zone, the state has two time zones.

10. Alaska has more time zones than the People's

Republic of China because Alaska has two time zones (the Alaska time zone and the Hawaii-Aleutian time zone), and the People's Republic of China has one time zone, Chinese Standard Time.

Quiz 15
Sports

1. What is the official national sport of Canada?

2. In what direction does the baseball pitch known as a curveball curve?

3. In what weight class did Muhammad Ali (Cassius Clay) fight during the 1960 Olympics?

4. How many consecutive strikes must a bowler throw to have a perfect game?

5. What sports personality originated the saying "Winning isn't everything. It's the only thing"?

6. Why did the first modern Olympics have a marathon race in 1896?

7. How did the word *seed* come to be used in tennis rankings?

8. During the 1980 Winter Olympics, America's hockey team, Team USA, received a gold medal immediately after defeating what country's team?

9. When pugilism is distinguished from boxing, what is the difference?

10. How did the San Diego Chargers get their name?

11. How did the Brooklyn Dodgers get their name?

12. Ever since its inception, the Rose Bowl has been held where?

Quiz 15 Answers
Sports

1. The official national sport of Canada is not ice hockey but lacrosse, which in 1867 was made the national game of Canada by the Canadian Parliament.

2. A curveball curves not sideways but downward. The curveball is really a drop ball and was called the "out drop" pitch in early baseball. When a curveball is thrown correctly, the hand will snap the ball over the index finger as it is released, spinning the ball from top to bottom and causing it to curve downward. Note that some pitches do curve sideways, but they aren't properly thrown curveballs. Rather, those are sliders, roundhouses, or improperly thrown curveballs.

3. Muhammad Ali (Cassius Clay) fought not as a heavyweight but as a light heavyweight in the 1960 Olympics.

4. A perfect game in bowling requires twelve strikes.

5. The sports personality on record for having *first* said "Winning isn't everything. It's the only thing" is not Vince Lombardi but Henry Russell (Red) Sanders, a former football coach at UCLA and Vanderbilt. Sanders uttered two versions on two different occasions. In 1950, at a Cal Poly San Luis Obispo physical education workshop, Sanders told his group: "Men, I'll be honest. Winning isn't everything. Men, it's the only thing." Those remarks were quoted in a *Los Angeles Times* article by Art Rosen-baum published on October 18, 1950. In 1955, in a *Sports Illustrated* article preceding the 1956 Rose Bowl, Sanders was quoted as saying, "Sure, winning isn't everything. It's the only thing." Vince Lombardi might have heard those words from Sanders and is on record using them as early as 1959 in Lombardi's opening-day talk for Packers' training camp. Even though the quotation came to be associated much more closely with Lombardi than with Sanders, Lombardi, according to James Michener's *Sports in America*, claimed to have been misquoted or at least misunderstood. He claimed that he had intended to say, "Winning isn't everything. The will to win is the only thing." Two facts are clear: Lombardi used the quotation on several occasions, and Red Sanders is on record for having used it before Lombardi. As a side note, this famous remark was repeated by a girl quoting John Wayne's character, a football coach, in the 1953 movie *Trouble Along the Way*.

6. The Olympic marathon, part of the modern Olympics, was not a race in the ancient Olympics. The origin of the twenty-six mile run stems from a heroic tale of fiction. Legend has it that a Greek messenger named Pheidippides ran twenty-six miles from Marathon to Athens to relate the victory of the Athenians over the Persians in 490 BCE. Right after delivering the message, Pheidippides died or so says the legend. The first three modern Olympic marathons, beginning in 1896, were roughly 26 miles, varying from game to game. In 1908, the distance became officially 26 miles and 385 yards. The games were then in London. The starting line for the marathon was outside a window at Windsor Castle, from which one half of the British Royal family could watch. The finish line was in front of the royal box in the White City stadium where the other half of the royal family was waiting. In short, the length of the modern marathon is due partly to an ancient legend and partly to the preferences of the British Royal family in 1908.

7. *Seed*, used in ranking tennis players in tournaments, comes from "conceded," referring to players who are conceded, or assumed, to be the best in ranking for a tournament. Casual usage led to *ceded*, which led to the current word *seed*.

8. Team USA received the gold medal for hockey not after defeating the Soviets but after defeating the Finns. Even though Team USA defeated the heavily favored Soviet team, which had not lost in the Olympics since 1960, the medal round was contested in a round-robin format. Consequently, even after defeating the Soviets, Team USA could have finished any position from first to fourth after the final game against Finland. It was only after the Americans defeated the Finns that America earned the gold medal. Note that the Finns placed fourth and so did not even receive a bronze medal, which went to Sweden. The Soviets, who received a silver medal, were disgraced, especially in the USSR, where the loss embarrassed the citizens. Ironically, Team USA had been beaten badly (ten to three) by the Soviets in a pre-Olympic exhibition game at New York's Madison Square Garden.

9. Pugilism, when it is distinguished from boxing, is bare-fisted. John L. Sullivan, then, engaged in pugilism.

10. The San Diego Chargers football team did not get their name from a charging style of play but from a business of the team's original owner, Barron Hilton, who owned the Carte Blanche credit card company and who, by the way, was the second son of Conrad Hilton, founder of Hilton Hotels.

11. The Brooklyn Dodgers were called Dodgers not because of their agility on the field but because of their being in Brooklyn, where Trolley Dodgers were Brooklynites living at the height of the trolley-car era, when there was a maze of trolley lines in the borough.

12. The Rose Bowl has always been held in Pasadena, California, *except* on January 1, 1942, when Duke and Oregon State met at Duke University because of security concerns just twenty-five days after the bombing of Pearl Harbor.

Quiz 16
Music/Instruments

1. How many performers were in the music group the Thompson Twins?

2. How many performers are in the music group Frankie Valli & the Four Seasons?

3. What kind of instrument (string, woodwind, percussion, and brass) is an English horn?

4. Who wrote the lyrics to "Stardust"?

5. Where was the rock group America formed?

6. How was the song "As Time Goes By" first introduced to the public?

7. Who wrote the Christmas carol "Away in a Manger"?

8. What British group created the first single record to reach number one on the U.S. Billboard Hot 100, beginning the British Invasion?

9. What is known as the Rolls-Royce of pianos?

10. What is the only acoustic (nonelectric) instrument invented in the twentieth century?

Quiz 16 Answers
Music/Instruments

1. The music group the Thompson Twins consisted of three performers, who were all unrelated.

2. The group Frankie Valli & the Four Seasons consists of four performers, including Valli.

3. An English horn is not a brass instrument; it is not a horn, and is not English. The English horn is an alto oboe (a woodwind) with an angled mouthpipe. The word *English* in English horn mistranslates the French for "angled."

4. The person who wrote the lyrics of "Stardust" was not Hoagy Carmichael, who wrote the music, but Mitchell Parish.

5. The rock group America was formed in England.

6. The song "As Time Goes By" was not introduced through the 1942 Warner movie *Casablanca* but in a 1931 musical called *Everybody's Welcome*.

7. Martin Luther did not write "Away in a Manger" but received credit for it because James R. Murray, its composer, wanted to help Luther spread Lutheranism.

8. The first group with a number one single was not

the Beatles but the Tornados, whose 1962 instrumental song "Telstar" began the British Invasion.

9. The Rolls-Royce of pianos is not a Steinway but the Bösendorfer Imperial Grand, manufactured only in Vienna.

10. The only acoustic instrument invented in the twentieth century was the steel pan drum, a tuned steel drum that can play more than one pitch. It was invented on the island of Trinidad and is strongly associated with Calypso music.

Quiz 17
Words

1. What is the English word for the central walkway in a church, down which the bride walks?

2. How did toadstools get their name?

3. What is the English word for the offspring of a female donkey and a stallion?

4. What was a pedagogue (Greek *paidagogos*) originally in ancient Greece?

5. What is the proper English word to describe a horse of either sex that is under one year of age?

6. In English, what is the name for a group of geese *in flight*?

7. Who is supposed to have been born by Immaculate Conception?

8. True or false: Many people have slid down banisters.

9. What is the singular of the word *graffiti*?

10. What is a vagina femoris?

11. What is a vagitus?

12. According to *The American Heritage Dictionary of the English Language*, how should you pronounce the color word *mauve*?

13. What is a vomitorium?

14. What is the Latin-derived term for a female graduate of a college or university?

15. How did Devil's Island, part of a French penal colony off the coast of French Guiana, get its name?

16. What does *madding* mean in the title *Far from the Madding Crowd*?

17. What is fulsome praise?

18. What is a specific English word for a group of kittens?

19. What is the correct two-word English phrase for self-belittling humor? *Hint:* It contains *self.*

20. How did we get the word *babble*?

21. What did *humble* in humble pie originally mean?

22. How should one pronounce *Pierre*, the capital of South Dakota?

23. What does *turdiform* mean?

24. What is an anal feeler?

25. What does *anile* mean?

26. What does *discomfit* mean?

27. How should one pronounce *Cannes*, the famous resort city on the French Riviera and home to the Cannes Film Festival?

28. How did the expression *drawing room* come into use?

29. What is a Hudson seal?

30. What is the traditional difference between dwarfs and midgets?

31. How did cesarean section get its name?

32. A civilian is a person who is not a member of what organization(s)?

33. In the former Soviet Union, to whom was the word *comrade* applied?

34. During what war was the expression *D-Day* first used?

35. In World War II, what did the *D* in *D-Day* stand for?

36. What is the word for the past tense of the verb *lie*, meaning "to recline"?

37. The verb *scan* can mean "to examine hastily or superficially." What else can it mean?

38. What is described by the noun *buttery*?

Quiz 17 Answers
Words

1. The English word for the central walkway in a church, down which the bride walks, is *nave*; the word *aisle* comes from Latin *ala* ("wing") and properly describes the side walkways in a church.

2. Toadstools have nothing to do with toads; rather, the often inedible and even poisonous fungi are called *toadstools* from the German *Tod* ("death") and *Stuhl* ("stool").

3. *Hinny* describes the offspring of a female donkey and a stallion. The word for the offspring of a male donkey and a mare is *mule*.

4. In ancient Greece, a pedagogue was not a teacher but a "leader of a boy"—that is, a slave who led a boy to school. It was in Latin that *paedagogus* came to mean "preceptor," a usage that passed into French and other modern languages.

5. A horse of either sex under one year of age is not called a colt (boy horse) or a filly (girl horse) but a foal.

6. The English word for a group of geese in flight is *skein*; the word *gaggle* describes geese on land or in water.

7. The person who some people believe had an Immaculate Conception was not Jesus, who was said to have had a virgin birth, but Mary, Jesus' mother, who, according to Roman Catholic doctrine, was purged of original sin at her conception.

8. The answer is false because no one slides down banisters; the part of the staircase people slide down is a balustrade, or handrail. Banisters are the uprights supporting the balustrade or handrail.

9. The singular of the word *graffiti* is *graffito*, from the Italian *graffito* ("scratching").

10. The vagina femoris is the connective tissue in muscles of the thigh.

11. A vagitus is the cry of a newborn child.

12. The word *mauve*, according to *The American Heritage Dictionary of the English Language* is pronounced *mōv*; in other symbols, *mohv*.

13. A vomitorium was not a place where ancient Romans or anyone else vomited or were permitted to vomit (or throw up) but was a passage situated below or behind a tier of seats in an amphitheater through which crowds could spew out at the end of some performance.

14. The Latin-derived term for a female graduate of a college or university is *alumna* (plural, *alumnae*).

15. Devil's Island got its name not from the penal conditions or the climate but from the turbulent waters surrounding it.

16. *Madding* does not mean "annoying" or "driving to insanity" but "frenzied." Thomas Hardy's title, by the way, was borrowed from poet Thomas Gray's "Elegy Written in a Country Churchyard."

17. Fulsome praise is excessive, insincere praise.

18. The specific English word for a group of kittens is not *litter*, which can designate animals of different kinds, but *kittle*, or *kindle*.

19. The two-word English phrase for self-belittling humor is not *self-deprecating humor*, which would be humor that is self-disapproving, but *self-depreciating humor*.

20. The English word *babble* has no clear and direct connection to the Tower of Babel (Genesis 11:4), which the Bible says is named from the Hebrew word for Babylon "because the Lord did there confound the language of all the earth" (Genesis 11:9), transforming the meaning of *Babel* by playing on the Hebrew word *balal* ("to confound"). The English word *babble* is probably an onomatopoeia—that is, a word that sounds like its meaning (like "sputter").

21. The origin of *humble* in *humble pie* relates not to the sense of "not proud" but to deer guts. It comes from *umble* or *numble*, designating the internal organs (heart, liver, kidneys, and intestines) of an animal such as a deer—parts more likely to be eaten by poor people than by wealthy people. Years ago, umbles were consumed reluctantly or unenthusiastically by servants, while their masters dined on venison.

22. The name of the capital of South Dakota, *Pierre*, should be pronounced as one syllable, like the word *peer*.

23. *Turdiform* means "like a thrush."

24. *Anal feeler* means "a posterior sensory appendage in worms and insects."

25. *Anile* means "pertaining to or like an elderly woman."

26. *Discomfit* does not mean "to discomfort" but "to make unsettled or confused" or "to thwart plans."

27. *Cannes* is pronounced not *kahn* but *kan*, like *can*, as in "a can of soup."

28. The expression *drawing room* did not come from any drawings that might or might not have existed in drawing rooms but in the rooms' use for withdrawing. The original expression was *withdrawing room*, describing a room in a home to which people could withdraw after dinner for conversation or relaxation.

29. Hudson seal is muskrat fur that is dyed, plucked, and sheared to resemble seal.

30. The word *dwarf* describes a person with shortened arms and legs, whereas *midget*, which is considered offensive, refers to a *little person* (the preferred expression) whose body is well proportioned, though smaller than average. There are numerous causes of dwarfism, including genetic ones, hormonal ones, and a combination of both.

31. Cesarean sections were not named after Julius Caesar but, in fact, existed before he was even born. The word *cesarean* derives from the Latin *cadre* ("to cut").

32. Strictly speaking, a civilian is someone who is not a member of some country's armed forces. Police officers of a city, town, or state are civilians, even though some of them call citizens who are not police *civilians*.

33. The world *comrade* was applied not to Soviet citizens generally but rather to members of the Communist Party.

34. Contrary to popular belief, the expression *D-Day* was first used during World War I. It described the attack at the St. Mihiel Salient, which began against German positions on September 12, 1918, in northeastern France. The battle, which ended on September 15, 1918, involved the American Expeditionary Force and 48,000 French soldiers under the command of U.S. General John J. Pershing.

35. During World War II, the *D* in *D-Day* stood for nothing. If one goes to the Internet and goes to the website called DOD Dictionary of Military Terms (www.dtic.mil/doctrine/dod_dictionary), one will see the definition of *D-Day* as the "unnamed day on which operations commence or are scheduled to commence."

36. The past tense of the verb *lie* (meaning "to recline") is *lay*, as in the title *As I Lay Dying*.

37. *Scan* can also mean "to examine minutely or carefully." The word *scan* is unusual because it has meanings that are contradictory. The word *cleave*, which can mean "to split" or "to join" is another word with contradictory meanings. Such words are sometimes called *contranyms*.

38. *Buttery* is not a room or pantry for storing butter. Rather, the word can be traced to the Middle English *boterie* ("ale cellar," "pantry"). Hence a buttery is a small room where food or alcohol is kept, though it can also describe a tea shop where students in British universities can buy light meals.

Inventors/Inventions

1. Who invented the guillotine?

2. Who founded the Gestapo (*Geheime Staatspolizei*), the Nazi secret state police?

3. Who invented the printing press, or movable type?

4. Who designed the German Autobahn?

5. Who started the first fire department in the United States?

6. What people invented kilts?

7. What is essential to an airship's being a dirigible?

8. Who invented the first heavier-than-air craft to make a sustained flight with its own power?

9. Who designed the Volkswagen?

10. Who invented the Franklin stove?

11. What was the first invention to go faster than the speed of sound (in air)?

12. Who invented the forward pass in football?

13. Which nation invented champagne?

14. What nation or culture produced the equal sign in mathematics?

15. Where was table tennis invented?

16. Who invented the military march called the goose step?

17. Who founded Mercedes-Benz?

18. In what country was the Sudoku puzzle invented?

19. Of electrician, furniture designer, dentist, and cardiologist, which was the occupation of the person who invented the electric chair?

20. What people first developed the potato?

21. Who invented the sandwich?

22. In what decade was the bikini invented?

23. Who invented the Bunsen burner?

24. Who invented the English expression *paleface* to describe white Europeans (as distinguished from American Indians)?

Quiz 18 Answers
Inventors/Inventions

1. The guillotine was invented not by Dr. Joseph-Ignace Guillotin, who encouraged the machine's use for painless death, but by Tobias Schmidt, a German mechanic under the direction of Dr. Antonin Louise, in honor of whom the guillotine was first known as a *Louison* or *Louisette*. In fact, there were guillotine-like devices in Europe centuries before the French Revolution.

2. The person who founded the Gestapo was not Heinrich Himmler, though he was head of the Gestapo for years, but rather Hermann Goering, who created it in 1933.

3. The Chinese were using movable type centuries before Johannes Gutenberg ever did. Gutenberg, however, was the first *European* to use it.

4. Neither Adolf Hitler nor the Third Reich cabinet invented the Autobahn. The Autobahn came into design twenty years before Hitler's reign and was implemented a year before Hitler came to power.

5. The first fire department in the United States was started not by Benjamin Franklin, who started the first fire department in Philadelphia, but by Peter (originally Pieter or Petrus) Stuyvesant, who in 1659 had buckets, ladders, and hooks distributed in New Amsterdam (a town on Manhattan Island renamed New York). By the way, among Stuyvesant's other accomplishments as director-general of New Amsterdam were the protective wall on Wall Street, the canal that became Broad Street, and Broadway.

6. Kilts were not originally Scottish but Irish.

7. A dirigible is distinguished by its capability of being directed and propelled through the air with the use of propellers and rudders (or other thrust).

8. The Wright Brothers were not the first to invent a heavier-than-air craft that could make a sustained flight under its own power; rather, the first inventor of such a craft was Samuel Pierpont Langley, whose Model No. 5, on May 6, 1896, flew for ninety seconds for about three quarters of a mile along the shore of the Potomac—a distance about ten times longer than that flown by any previous heavier-than-air flying machine. Driven by a one-horsepower steam engine and weighing only twenty-six pounds, the passengerless plane gently descended, was refueled, and relaunched the same afternoon. The Wright Brothers are, however, given credit for achieving the first flight to carry a human passenger, at Kitty Hawk, North Carolina, on December 17, 1903.

9. The person who designed the Volkswagen was Ferdinand Porsche, though engineer Béla Barényi is at times credited with having conceived the basic design for the Volkswagen Beetle in 1925, five years before Porsche claimed to have completed his version. Barényi, by the way, was inducted into the Detroit Automobile Hall of

Fame in 1994 and is often regarded as the father of passive safety in automobiles.

10. The inventor of the Franklin stove was not Benjamin Franklin but David R. Rittenhouse, astronomer, inventor, clockmaker, mathematician, surveyor, and public official. Franklin invented the Pennsylvania Fireplace, which was designed to draw smoke from the bottom rather than from the top. Unfortunately, the smoke didn't defy the laws of heat convection. In short, hot air rises, so Franklin's stove was, of course, ineffective. David R. Rittenhouse redesigned the stove in the 1790s by adding an L-shaped exhaust pipe to vent the smoke. Even though Rittenhouse renamed the stove the Rittenhouse stove, it came to be known as the Franklin stove.

11. The first invention to go faster than the speed of sound (in air) was the whip, invented in China thousands of years ago. A whip's crack is produced by a loop that forms in the whip as one flicks it. The loop travels the length of the whip, speeding up as it moves and producing a small sonic boom.

12. The forward pass was not invented by Notre Dame under Knute Rockne, though Notre Dame used it with devastating effect against Army at West Point in 1913. The forward pass had been legal since 1906 and had been used by many teams over conservative objections. In fact, a remarkably versatile athlete and coach, Amos Alonzo Stagg, claimed in 1906 that he had dozens of pass plays in his repertoire. What's more, Walter Camp, the father of American football, was the first to propose the forward pass to the rules committee, though it was adopted under severe restrictions. For example, failure to complete a pass resulted in a fifteen-yard penalty from the spot where the ball was put into play and the loss of a down.

13. Champagne was not invented by the French but by the English. In the sixteenth century, the English imported barrels of green, flat wine from Champagne, France, and added sugar and molasses to begin fermentation. What's more, they developed corks and coal-fired glass bottles to contain it. According to the records of the Royal Society in 1662, *méthode Champenoise* was first written down in England. Contrary to what some people think, the Benedictine monk Dom Pérignon (1638–1715) did not invent champagne but spent much of his time trying to remove the bubbles.

14. The equal sign was not invented by the Greeks, the Babylonians, or the Arabs but by a Welsh astronomer and mathematician Robert Recorde in 1557. A child prodigy, Recorde wrote popular math textbooks, introduced algebra to an English audience, and introduced the equal sign (=).

15. Table tennis was invented not in China but in England, where it was originally played with balls made from champagne corks and paddles from cigar-box lids. English engineer James Gibb introduced a celluloid ball. The name *Ping-Pong* was originally trademarked in 1901 by a British company that made sports equipment. The trademark was later sold to Parker Brothers, and, as of 2009, is owned by Escalade Sports. Technically, Olympic athletes play table tennis, not Ping-Pong.

16. The goose step military march was invented not by the Nazis but by Prussian generals in the 1600s. The goose step was adopted by the Russians in the twentieth century and is still used in some countries of the Middle East and in North Korea.

17. Mercedes-Benz was not founded by anyone named Mercedes. An Austrian employed by the Daimler car company, Emil Jellinek, had a daughter, Mercedes, after whom he named an engine and several racing cars. The name Benz comes from Karl Benz, an auto manufacturer whose company merged with Daimler in 1926, creating the brand name Mercedes-Benz. In 1998, the name Daimler resurfaced when the company merged with the Chrysler Corporation to form Daimler-Chrysler.

18. Sudoku was invented in America. Sudoku, despite its name, was invented in the 1970s by a retired architect from Indianapolis named Howard Garns. The logic puzzles were originally called Number Place Puzzles and were published by Dell in a magazine for children. Rediscovered in the 1980s by the Japanese puzzle publisher Nikoli, the puzzles were renamed *Suuji wa dokushin ni kagiru* ("the numbers must occur only once"). To cope with a cumbersome name, the publisher abbreviated it to Sudoku. The puzzles gained increasing popularity in Japan and, by 2005, became popular throughout the world, rivaling even crossword puzzles in popularity.

19. The person who invented the electric chair was a dentist. In 1881, Dr. Alfred Southwick (1826–1898), a dentist from Buffalo, New York, saw an intoxicated man touch a live electric generator, which quickly killed him.

Dr. Southwick concluded that electricity could be used as an alternative to hanging as capital punishment. Because he was a dentist and was used to dealing with subjects in chairs, his device for electrical execution took the form of an electric chair. Working with David B. Hill, then-governor of New York State, Dr. Southwick achieved his goal of making execution by electricity legal. He also served on the state's Electrical Death Commission, which between 1888 and 1889 recommended electrocution for capital punishment. On January 1, 1889, the first law allowing the use of electrocution went into effect. On August 6, 1890, William Kemmler, who had butchered his mistress with a hatchet, achieved the distinction of being the first person to be killed by an electric chair. He, by the way, was exposed to electric current twice. His first exposure, which lasted seventeen seconds, left him unconscious but breathing. The embarrassed prison officials tried to electrocute him again, this time for seventy seconds, causing him to thrash and convulse and searing his head and arms. Some witnesses fainted while others fled the room. The killing took about eight minutes. Dr. Southwick, who witnessed the execution, was reported to have said, "We live in a higher civilization from this day."

20. The first people to develop the potato were not Irish but Peruvians. The potato is from a species in the *Solanum brevicaule* complex. Although Peru is the birthplace of the potato, today nearly all cultivated potatoes worldwide are descendants of a subspecies indigenous to Chile. The potato was introduced to Europe in the 1530s, where it became an important crop and food staple. Because very few varieties were initially introduced, the

European crop had little genetic diversity and was vulnerable to disease. In 1845, a plant disease known as late blight spread rapidly through poor communities of western Ireland, producing a crop failure that led to the Irish potato famine.

21. The inventor of the sandwich was not John Montagu, the earl of Sandwich, who wanted to eat while playing cards. The fact is, Arabs were stuffing meats into pita bread centuries before Montagu was born, and European peasants working in fields ate meals of bread and cheese. Ancient Jews, furthermore, ate sandwiches of nuts and fruit placed between matzo during the Passover seder. The earl of Sandwich, however, was the person after whom the Sandwich Islands (now Hawaii) were once named.

22. In 1946, two Frenchmen, Jacques Heim and Louis Réard, invented what was called the bikini, but scanty two-piece swimsuits existed long before then. When the bikini was invented, the U.S. Army was testing nuclear weapons on the Bikini Atoll. The inventors of the bikini hoped their new item would be as *explosive* in the fashion world.

23. The Bunsen burner was not invented by its namesake Robert Wilhelm Bunsen, who introduced and popularized the burner in 1855. Although no one knows for sure, many believe that either Peter Desdega or Michael Faraday was its true inventor.

24. American Indians most likely did not coin the word *paleface*, which was most likely invented and was definitely popularized by white Americans. The one American who did the most to popularize the expression was James Fenimore Cooper (1789–1851), whose book *The Last of the Mohicans* (1826) made *paleface* a household word. According to Answers.com, there exists an 1822 report of a frontier masquerade party where a white man dressed as an Indian chief says to another white man, "Ah, Paleface! What brings you here? You seem to take pleasure in saying rude impertinencies." Even if the word existed before *The Last of the Mohicans*, there is no good evidence that Indians originated it.

Quiz 19
Hodgepodge

1. What color is the white rhinoceros?

2. What was the usual color of mourning in the Far East, ancient Rome, and Sparta?

3. What color are you if you're livid?

4. The first Ford Model Ts came in what color or colors?

5. What color are black bears?

6. What was the shape of Viking helmets?

7. What color is the black box on a commercial airplane?

8. When pirates wanted to dispose of their captives, how did they dispose of them?

9. What causes the cracking sound that occurs after the thumb and middle finger are snapped together?

10. Of Wilbur Wright, President William Howard Taft, Paul Newman, and President James Garfield, who *wasn't* born in Ohio?

11. How do bit parts, cameos, extras, and walk-ons differ?

12. What do St. Bernards carry around their necks?

13. Why are no letters assigned to the digits one and zero on a telephone keypad?

14. According to the World Health Organization, what disease or substance is responsible for the death of one in ten adults worldwide?

15. What is an igloo?

16. What is the name of the large, branched candlestick, or holder for lights, such as the one used by the pianist Liberace? *Hint:* The word starts with *can-*.

17. In the nineteenth century, covered bridges were particularly popular; why were they preferred to ordinary bridges?

18. What was the worst maritime disaster, judged by the number of fatalities?

19. How can people cure split ends?

20. What is the connection between the U.S. Interstate Highway System and aviation (or aircraft landings)?

21. For what work did Albert Einstein receive the Nobel Prize for physics in 1921?

22. In what discipline did parapsychological researcher Dr. J. B. Rhine receive his graduate degree?

23. What's the radiance surrounding the head or figure of saints in paintings?

24. What is the name of James Whistler's most famous painting, which is of his mother?

25. What did the artist van Gogh do to one of his ears?

26. In May 1970, which Americans were more likely to disapprove of the Vietnam War, those in their twenties or those ages fifty or older?

27. What was the original reason for brides' carrying bouquets of strong-smelling herbs, garlic, and chives?

28. When is Boxing Day celebrated as a holiday in parts of the British Commonwealth, during which Christmas gifts are given to service workers?

29. From what is a camel-hair brush made?

30. From what wood was Howard Hughes's *Spruce Goose* made?

31. What is rice paper made from?

32. What's in German silver?

33. In the 1931 movie *Frankenstein*, what is the name of the monster?

34. In what month was the famous Christmas movie *Miracle on 34th Street* released in 1947?

35. Who sketched and animated Mickey Mouse?

36. What movie star said "Drop the gun, Louie"?

37. What actor said "Judy, Judy, Judy!"?

38. In the United States, is it possible to be legally tried twice for the same action?

39. What is true about a United States ship captain's legal right to conduct weddings?

40. How many phone calls may one make from a U.S. jail?

41. How might one distinguish an attorney from an attorney-at-law?

42. What make of motorcycle did Marlon Brando have in the film *The Wild One*?

Quiz 19 Answers
Hodgepodge

1. The white rhinoceros, like the black rhinoceros, is gray-brown. "White," a corruption of the Afrikaans word *wijd* ("wide"), refers to the animal's lips. The black rhinoceros is distinguished by its pointed upper lip, which it uses for browsing on thorny bushes. The white rhinoceros, however, feeds on grass.

2. The usual color of mourning in the Far East, in ancient Rome, and in Sparta was white.

3. If you are livid, you are not red but ashen.

4. Many Model T Fords came in black, though the cars originally came in other colors, such as Brewster green, red, blue, and gray. In fact, during its first year, Model T Fords weren't available in black at all but only in gray, red, and green. It is often said that Ford chose black because the paint dried faster than other paints available at the time, and a faster drying paint would speed production time. The fact is that more than thirty types of black paint were used to paint different parts of the Model T, and the different paints had different drying times. Ford engineering documents suggest that the color black was chosen because it was inexpensive and durable. No one, by the way, can conclusively prove that Henry Ford ever said that the buying public could have Model T Fords in any color, so long as it was black, but we do know that from 1914 to 1925 all Model Ts came only in black.

5. Black bears are usually black but possibly white or cream (as on Kermode Island and its vicinity in British Columbia), or brown, or cinnamon (in south-central Alaska and the southeastern mainland) or blue or glacier (in the Yakutat area of southeast Alaska). In fact, about 20 percent of black bears are not black. A black bear, by the way, can have a patch of white on its chest. Black bears, the smallest of the three species of North American bears, are also the most abundant and widely distributed and are seen in every state except Hawaii.

6. The Vikings wore helmets, but the helmets were not horned. Horned helmets were used in Celtic religious rituals but were unsuitable for combat because the horns could have been easily caught on weapons. The imagery of horned Vikings is thought to stem from nineteenth-century Scandinavism, a romantic nationalist movement.

7. The color of the black box is orange, which is much easier to see than black, especially among wreckage.

8. Pirates did not dispose of their captives by making the captives walk the plank (a myth) but by throwing them overboard.

9. The sound that occurs after the thumb and middle finger are snapped is caused not by the forceful connection of the thumb and the middle finger but by the middle finger's striking the base of thumb.

10. Wilbur Wright was not born in Ohio but Millville, Indiana; his brother, Orville, was born in Dayton, Ohio. Ohio is sometimes called the Birthplace of Aviation.

11. A bit part is a small role for a supporting actor, calling for at least one line of a dialogue. A cameo (or cameo appearance) is a brief appearance of a famous person (often not an actor) in a movie, play, or TV show, as in Alfred Hitchcock's cameos in more than thirty of his movies. An extra is an anonymous person appearing in a nonspeaking role, usually in the background as a pedestrian, a patron of a restaurant, or a person sitting on a bench. A walk-on is marginally more important than an extra because a walk-on is clearly seen, usually performing some easily identifiable action, such as taking an order at a restaurant or writing someone a parking ticket.

12. St. Bernards have never carried brandy barrels around their necks. Before they were trained as rescue dogs, St. Bernards carried food for the monks at the hospice in the Great St. Bernard Pass, the alpine route linking Switzerland to Italy. The mistaken belief that St. Bernards carry brandy can be traced to a Victorian painter of landscapes and animals named Sir Edwin Landseer (1802–1873), who painted a scene called *Alpine Mastiff: Reanimating a Distressed Traveler*, which features two St. Bernards, one of which carried a miniature brandy barrel around its neck, added "for interest." Although the monastery has come to use helicopters rather than

St. Bernards to rescue people, it is estimated that the dogs have made more than 25,000 rescues since 1800.

13. The digits zero and one remain without letters on telephones because they are *flag* numbers, kept for special purposes, such as emergencies or operator services.

14. The substance responsible for the death of one in ten adults worldwide is tobacco. If figures continue to rise at current levels, tobacco use and consequent smoking-related diseases will become the leading cause of unnatural deaths in the world by 2030, when tobacco is predicted to be implicated in the deaths of about ten million people a year.

15. Strictly speaking, the word *igloo* (or iglu) does not necessarily designate a rounded Eskimo house made from blocks of ice; rather, the word means "house" in Inuit. Most igloos are made of stone or hide. The precursors of the Inuit, the Thule, did live in snow-block igloos, which were used in central and eastern Canada. Although Canadian Eskimos built igloos from snow, snow-block igloos are not built in Alaska. Few, in fact, exist anywhere today.

16. The large, branched candlestick is called a *candelabrum*, not a *candelabra* (a plural form that would describe two or more).

17. The main reason covered bridges were preferred to ordinary bridges was to protect the bridge from exposure to the elements, not to protect travelers. Early bridges were often made of wood, making them more likely to deteriorate within only ten years. Covering them protected their structural members, extending their usefulness for decades.

18. The deadliest maritime disaster was not the 1912 sinking of the *Titanic*, which killed more than 1,500 people, but the sinking of the MV *Wilhelm Gustloff*, a German passenger ship sunk by a Russian submarine in 1945 in the Baltic Sea, killing at least 5,000 people and possibly more than 9,000. The Russians sank the ship, which was evacuating civilian refugees, German soldiers, and U-boat personnel surrounded by the Red Army in what was then East Prussia.

19. Strictly speaking, people cannot cure or mend split ends by applying some hair care product, though they can get haircuts or shave their heads. Once the cuticle of the hair shaft is split, it can often grow split, but it cannot be mended. What some hair care products do is not mend split ends but soften hair texture by using fillers that attach to the hair shaft.

20. It is false that the U.S. Interstate Highway System was designed so that every five (or ten) miles can accommodate emergency or military aircraft landings. Although the federal government is capable of wastefulness, it is unlikely that legislators behind the highway system would have supported interrupting the flow of troops, supplies, and civilians during domestic crises to land planes, especially when a large number of major airports, private airstrips, military airstrips, or American aircraft carriers could be used for the same purpose. Richard Weingroff, information liaison specialist for the Federal Highway Administration's Office of Infrastructure and its unofficial historian, asserts that the closest the myth came to reality occurred in 1944, when Congress briefly considered funding emergency landing strips in the Federal Highway-Aid Act, authorizing a National System of Interstate Highways. The highways themselves were never considered potential airstrips; rather, the proposed landing strips would have been built alongside major highways, enabling ground transportation to and from the strips. The proposal, however, was dropped. Many people who believe in the one-mile-in-five assertion claim that it was part of the Federal Aid Highway Act of 1956, committing the federal government to build what became the 42,800-mile Interstate Highway System (officially called the *Dwight D. Eisenhower National System of Interstate and Defense Highways*). That act did not, however, specify anything related to emergency landing strips, nor did it mention any one-mile-in-five requirements.

21. Albert Einstein received his Nobel Prize in physics not for the theory of relativity, published sixteen years earlier, but for Einstein's lesser-known work on the photoelectric effect of light.

22. Dr. Joseph Banks Rhine, who founded the parapsychology lab at Duke University and the *Journal of Parapsychology*, earned his graduate degree in botany, not psychology.

23. The radiance surrounding the head or figure of saints in paintings is not a halo but a nimbus. The word *halo* is a general term for any disc or luminosity (including the ring seen around the sun during an eclipse); the word *nimbus* specifically refers to the radiance surrounding godlike figures walking the Earth.

24. The official name of James Whistler's most famous painting is not *Whistler's Mother* but *Arrangement in Grey and Black, No. 1: Portrait of the Painter's Mother*, which he later renamed *Portrait of My Mother*.

25. Van Gogh did not cut off his entire ear or even most of it; he cut off an earlobe and a bit more. On Christmas Eve, 1888, he grabbed a razor and chased the painter Gauguin, with whom van Gogh was having strained relations and arguing. Van Gogh ended up using the razor on himself, according to him, because of remorse, though possibly also or alternatively to relieve his tinnitus (ringing in the ear). After cutting off the lobe and a bit more, he wrapped the severed body part in a newspaper and gave it to a local prostitute he loved named Rachel, whom he asked to take good care of it. As a result of van Gogh's irrational violence, Gauguin never spoke with him again, and the authorities placed van Gogh in an asylum.

26. Although many young people in the 1960s were vocally opposed to the Vietnam War and demonstrated against it, opinion polling in the United States showed that younger people were more likely to support sending United States troops to Vietnam than older people were. According to the Pew Research Center for the People and the Press, by May 1970, 49 percent of young people thought that the Vietnam War was a mistake, whereas, 61 percent of those age fifty or older thought that it was a mistake, and 53 percent of those age thirty to forty-nine believed that it was a mistake. In short, even during the height of anti-Vietnam sentiment, Americans fifty or older were more likely to disapprove of the war than those under thirty.

27. The original reason brides carried bouquets of strong-smelling herbs, garlic, and chives was to ward off evil spirits.

28. Boxing Day is not necessarily December 26, but the first weekday after Christmas, which can be December 26 or later.

29. A camel-hair brush does not use camel hair but the hair of any number of other animals, including goats, squirrels, sheep, bears, and ponies.

30. The *Spruce Goose* was not made from spruce but from birch. The name *Spruce Goose* was commonly given to several all-wood airplanes. Although many news reports and airplane enthusiasts liked the term for Hughes's plane, he did not. Built at a reported cost of $40 million and designed to carry several hundred soldiers, the huge plane flew only one time (November 2, 1947), for about one thousand yards at a height of seventy feet.

31. Rice paper (or pith paper) comes not from rice but from the pith of the so-called rice paper plant (*Tetrapanax papyriferus*).

32. German silver is not silver but an alloy of mostly copper, zinc, and nickel.

33. The name of the monster in the 1931 movie was not Frankenstein, the creator's name. In the movie *Frankenstein*, the monster has no name.

34. The Christmas movie *Miracle on 34th Street* was originally released not in December but in July. Neither the producer Darryl F. Zanuck nor the other 20th Century executives intended it to be a Christmas movie.

35. The person who sketched and animated Mickey Mouse was not Walt Disney but Ub Iwerks, Disney's chief animator in the early days of the studio.

36. Nobody, including Humphrey Bogart, in Casablanca, ever said, "Drop the gun, Louie." Instead, Bogart said, "Not so fast, Louie."

37. No actor seriously said in a movie, "Judy, Judy, Judy," but Cary Grant did say, in the 1939 *Only Angels Have Wings*, "Hello Judy," "Come on, Judy," and "Now, Judy." In the 1938 movie, *Bringing Up Baby*, Cary Grant does say "Susan, Susan, Susan."

38. People can be tried twice for the same act if the act violated both federal and state law. The Fifth Amendment to the U.S. Constitution prohibits double jeopardy in federal cases. The U.S. Supreme Court, however, in 1922 held that someone could be tried in federal court for a federal offense and then in state court for a state statute. Note also, by the way, that the double jeopardy prohibition didn't apply to O.J. Simpson's situation because he received only one criminal trial for homicide; the other trial involving homicide was a civil trial. O.J. Simpson couldn't legally be retried, in a criminal court, for the charges of homicide, of which he had already been acquitted.

39. U.S. ship captains may not perform weddings unless they are specifically authorized to do so because of their being priests, rabbis, ministers, judges, or justices of the peace. Indeed, some U.S. maritime regulations prohibit ship captains from conducting wedding ceremonies.

40. Americans in jail are entitled to make as many as they need to get in touch with lawyers and to conduct legal matters.

41. Strictly speaking, an attorney need not be an attorney-at-law but is someone legally authorized to act on behalf of another, as in power-of-attorney. A person authorized to make medical decisions on behalf of another can be said to be an attorney. An attorney-at-law is someone professionally trained in the law who is authorized to give legal advice or represent another in court. An attorney who is a lawyer is an attorney-at-law.

42. The motorcycle Marlon Brando had in *The Wild One* was a 1950 Triumph 6T Thunderbird, not a Harley-Davidson, the make Lee Marvin had.

Quiz 20
Botany

1. On what sort of plant do bananas grow?

2. What is the common name of the flower known as fleur-de-lis (lys)?

3. What are coffee beans?

4. What liquid is inside a coconut?

5. Of blackberries, strawberries, blueberries, and raspberries, which are true berries?

6. Of the following plants, which are not seeds—peanuts, navy beans, rice, corn, or tapioca?

7. What happens when you scratch skin with poison ivy and then touch another part of your body?

8. How often do century plants bloom?

9. What is the world's oldest single living organism?

10. What is misleading about the proposition that autumn leaves change color from green to yellow and orange?

Quiz 20 Answers
Botany

1. Bananas do not grow on trees but on very large herbs, which contain no roots and have woodless "trunks" consisting of false stems made up of large sheaths wrapped together.

2. The fleur-de-lis is not a lily (as commonly thought) but an iris.

3. Coffee beans are not beans, which are the seeds or pods of certain leguminous plants used mainly for food, but are the seeds or pits of a red, cherry-like fruit.

4. The liquid inside a coconut is not coconut milk, which is produced from boiling the white coconut meat with water and straining it, but coconut water, which is full of vitamins and minerals and has the same balance of salts as human blood.

5. Of the fruits mentioned, only blueberries are true berries. Blackberries, raspberries, and strawberries are aggregated drupes. Drupes are fleshy fruits containing a single stone or pit. The fruits mentioned are called *aggregated drupes* because each individual fruit is a cluster of miniature drupes (bumpy bits making up the fruit).

6. Of the plants listed, the only one that does not consist of seeds is the tapioca, which is made from the root of the cassava plant.

7. The symptoms of poison ivy aren't spread by scratching the body. Some parts of the body can show symptoms before other parts, but the difference in the appearance of those symptoms is due to the variable thickness of the skin. It takes more time for the plant's toxic oil to soak into areas of thicker skin. What's more, the liquid in poison ivy blisters doesn't contain the toxic oil. Consequently, you can't spread poison ivy by breaking blisters. Because it takes about fifteen minutes for the oil to soak into the surface of the skin, you'd do well to wash your skin with soap and water as soon as possible after exposure.

8. The succulent known as the century plant belongs to the genus *Agave*. Although it blooms infrequently, it doesn't require a hundred years. Plants belonging to the *Agave* family can bloom in various spans of time, depending on the species. Some may bloom in one year; some may bloom in as many as fifty years; still others may take more or less time to bloom.

9. The oldest living single organism is a tree, though not a sequoia; rather; it is a bristlecone pine, which can be found in California, Colorado, New Mexico, Arizona, Utah, and Nevada. The oldest single living organism is a particular bristlecone pine nicknamed Methuselah in the Ancient Bristlecone Pine Forest in the White Mountains of eastern California. In 1957, Methuselah was determined to be 4,789 years old, 3,820 years older than its biblical namesake. There are, by the way, some plants (such as the creosote bush) forming clonal colonies that may be several times older than bristlecone pines. The existing growth in clonal colonies sprang as shoots from older growth, creating an unbroken chain of life dating back tens of thousands of years. Nonetheless, the original ancient growth in those clonal colonies is long dead, making the oldest bristlecone pines the oldest single continuously living organisms.

10. Although leaves appear to change color from green to yellow and orange in the fall, the yellow and orange pigments (carotenoids) seen in autumn foliage were already there, but they were hidden under the green pigment (chlorophyll). When the chlorophyll breaks down, it disappears, exposing the yellow and orange pigments. The bright reds and purples seen on, for example, sugar maples, however, aren't unveiled in the way that yellow and orange are; instead, the reds and purples are produced by sunlight striking glucose stored in the leaves.

Physics

1. In what direction will a passenger's head be thrown in a head-on collision?

2. Air is composed primarily of what gas?

3. Which is faster, the speed of sound in air or the speed of sound in water?

4. What color is water?

5. Does bumblebee flight contradict the laws of thermodynamics?

6. Does battery current flow from the negative electrode to the positive electrode or from the positive electrode to the negative electrode?

7. What is the speed of light?

8. True or false: Glass is a high-viscosity liquid at room temperature.

9. Why would a person place a teaspoon in the neck of an opened bottle of champagne?

10. True or false: Water in a sink or toilet rotates

counterclockwise in the Northern Hemisphere and clockwise in the Southern Hemisphere because of the Coriolis Effect, caused by the rotation of Earth.

Quiz 21 Answers
Physics

1. A passenger's head in a head-on collision will not be thrown back but forward. Because a moving body will continue to move in the same direction unless met by an opposing force, a human body in a forward-moving vehicle will continue to move forward if the vehicle is brought to a sudden halt. If the drivers aren't restrained by seat belts or air bags, their heads may strike steering wheels or windshields. Only if a vehicle is struck from the rear, or it strikes an object while moving in reverse, is there a chance that the driver's neck will snap back enough to cause true whiplash.

2. Air consists mostly of nitrogen (about 78 percent).

3. The speed of sound in water is faster than the speed of sound in air. The speed of sound describes how much distance a sound wave travels in some specified medium. In dry air at 68°F, the speed of sound is 767 mph or about one mile in five seconds. The speed is highly dependent on air temperature but almost independent of air pressure or density. Sound travels faster in liquids and nonporous solids than in air. In fact, sound travels about 4.4 times faster in water than in air.

4. The color of water is an extremely faint blue. The blue color is visible through the ice of a frozen waterfall. The water can appear to be strikingly blue when people look at it rather than through it because of the reflected color from the sky. In seas and lakes, algae and microscopic plants will affect the appearance of the water. When particles reflect and scatter the light as it returns to the surface, the water can appear to be different colors, including green, like the Mediterranean.

5. Bumblebees obviously can fly, and their flight violates no scientific laws. In the past, some people, including some scientists, were puzzled by the flight of the bumblebee. Such people believed that its wings are too small, its body too big, and its muscles too weak to support flight. Some say the mystery of the bumblebee began with researchers in aerodynamics in the 1930s who viewed bumblebee wings as static airfoils, without having the necessary lift to get the insect's mass airborne. Bumblebee wings, however, are not static but mobile, producing lift by moving through the air in many directions. In fact, the wings oscillate about two hundred times per second. Bumblebees resemble helicopters more than airplanes, and the flight of the bumblebee is, therefore, explicable.

6. A battery current flows from the negative electrode to the positive electrode. When a battery cell operates, the negative electrode gives up electrons to an external circuit, and the positive electrode accepts electrons from the external circuit.

7. The speed of light is not constant except in a vacuum. The speed of light *in a vacuum* is 299,792.458 meters per second or roughly 186,282,397 miles per second. That speed is about a million times faster than the speed of sound in air. The fastest speed light actually travels, however, is roughly 670,616,629.4 miles per hour. At such speed, sunlight takes about 8.3 minutes to reach Earth. The speed of electromagnetic waves slows down as they pass through matter. How much light slows down depends on the nature of the medium through which it passes. The speed of light through diamonds, for example, is about 80,000 miles per second, about half as fast as it moves in a vacuum.

8. The proposition is false because glass is not a high-viscosity liquid but an amorphous solid, a solid in which there is no long-range order of the positions of the atoms. Most classes of solid materials can be found or prepared in an amorphous form, including many polymers and even foods such as cotton candy. People who think that glass is a high-viscosity liquid note that panes of stained glass windows often have thicker glass at the bottom than at the top. That unevenness, however, is due not to the movement of the glass but to the unevenness of the glass when it was installed. It is fairly common to find old windows that are thicker at the sides or the tops.

9. People who place spoons in the necks of opened champagne bottles believe—erroneously—that a teaspoon will help the champagne retain its carbonation. There is no good empirical evidence for that belief. Because many people believe that the practice will work, they may, however, perceive it as effective, especially in the absence of any scientific test.

10. The proposition about the drainage of water is false. The Coriolis Effect is the inertial force that deflects an object (such as air masses) moving about Earth. The deflection is rightward in the Northern Hemisphere and leftward in the Southern Hemisphere. In an episode of *The Simpsons* "Bart vs. Australia," Lisa tells Bart that toilets in the Northern Hemisphere (for example, America) drain counterclockwise, whereas those in the Southern Hemisphere drain clockwise. Lisa is incorrect. Although the Coriolis Effect influences the movement of ocean currents and air masses in the atmosphere, it is negligible in affecting the water that runs down toilets and bathtub and sink drains. What determines the direction of drainage is principally the shape of the basin and the direction from which it was filled.

Quiz 22
Slang

1. In slang, what is German tea?

2. In slang, what are Russian boots?

3. In slang, what are Mexican strawberries?

4. In slang, what is a Chinese fire drill?

5. In slang, what is a Spanish fiddle?

6. In slang, what is a Turkish medal?

7. In slang, what is an Arizona tenor?

8. In slang, what is a Scotch organ?

9. In slang, what is Italian perfume?

10. In slang, what is a Dutch feast?

11. In slang, what is a Dutch nightingale?

12. What is a bunghole borer?

13. What is blowing the grampus?

Quiz 22 Answers
Slang

1. In slang, *German tea* describes beer.

2. In slang, *Russian boots* describes leg irons.

3. In slang, the phrase *Mexican strawberries* describes beans.

4. In slang, *Chinese fire drill* describes chaos or a situation in which everyone gets out of a car when it's stopped at a traffic light, runs around it, and gets back in a different seat.

5. In slang, *Spanish fiddle* describes a crosscut saw.

6. In slang, *Turkish medal* describes an unbuttoned fly.

7. In slang, *Arizona tenor* describes a cougher (who has gone to the southwest for reasons of health).

8. In slang, *Scotch organ* describes a cash register.

9. In slang, *Italian perfume* describes garlic.

10. In slang, *Dutch feast* describes a dinner at which the host gets drunk before or after the guests arrive.

11. In slang, *Dutch nightingale* describes a frog.

12. A *bunghole borer* is one who operates a machine that bores holes in casks or barrels.

13. *Blowing the grampus* describes the tradition of throwing a bucket of cold water on a sailor who has been asleep while on watch.

Quiz 23

Insects and Related Things

1. What do moths do to clothes?

2. What do bees collect from flowers?

3. How do crickets chirp?

4. What sort of creature is a daddy longlegs?

5. How dangerous is tarantula venom to human beings?

6. Which creature has killed the most human beings?

7. What will dragonflies do to human beings?

8. What do female mosquitoes do to people that is irritating?

9. How do most tree worms get into apples?

10. What are male bees called?

Insects and Related Things

1. Moths do little or nothing to clothes, and they don't eat them. The damage found in wool and fur is done when the eggs of moths hatch and the larvae begin feeding on clothes. After feeding, the larvae will eventually form cocoons, change into moths, and then fly away to repeat the cycle.

2. Bees do not collect honey from flowers; they collect nectar, which is converted into honey by other bees in the hive.

3. Crickets chirp not by rubbing their legs together, but by rubbing a scraper on one forewing along a row of 50 to 250 teeth on an opposite forewing.

4. A daddy longlegs is not a spider or an insect. Although a daddy longlegs has eight legs like a spider, it isn't a spider. While daddy longlegs, like scorpions, ticks, mites, and spiders, belong to the class Arachnida, the daddy longlegs belongs to the separate order Phalangida; spiders belong to the order Araneida.

5. Though they look scary and have a fearsome reputation, tarantulas have bites that are often no more harmful than wasp stings and aren't fatal. Accounts of bites by tarantulas of some species, however, are reported to be painful. What's more, some people can suffer severe symptoms because of allergic reactions to proteins included in the venom.

6. The creature most deadly to human beings is the mosquito, which carries disease-causing viruses and parasites from person to person without catching the diseases itself. Mosquitoes can transmit many diseases, including encephalitis, but they are especially known for producing yellow fever, dengue fever, and malaria. Mosquitoes are estimated to transmit disease to more than seven hundred million people annually in Africa, South America, Central America, Mexico, and much of Asia, killing millions of people.

7. Contrary to popular opinion, dragonflies don't sting, though their larvae (nymphs) can bite. By the way, dragonflies are among the fastest flying insects, if not the fastest.

8. Female mosquitoes do not bite but pierce their victims with a long hollow tube (a proboscis), through which they suck blood. Before the female mosquito extracts blood, she injects an anticoagulant to prevent the blood from clotting. The itchy bumps people get from mosquito "bites" are allergic reactions to the anticoagulant. The mosquito gets blood not to eat but to nourish eggs. Mosquitoes feed on nectar and other plant juices.

9. The usual way in which tree worms get into apples is not by boring into the apples but by being born in them. After a fruit fly punctures a growing apple and plants its eggs in the hole, the eggs hatch and release tiny white worms that grow as they eat the apple tissue. After the apple falls to the ground, the worms crawl out the apple and develop into fruit flies.

10. Male bees are drones; female bees are workers—unless they are queens.

Quiz 24
Measurements

1. How many pounds are in a British hundredweight?

2. In Britain, France, and Germany, a billion is how many million?

3. What are the dimensions of the familiar lumber known as a 2×4 (a two by four)?

4. According to the U.S. government and its mints, what is the coin whose value is 1/100 of a dollar?

5. What percentage of the brain do people use?

6. What is relative humidity?

7. Roughly, how much water would a ten-gallon hat hold?

8. What weighs more, a pound of feathers or a pound of gold?

9. Roughly, what percentage of heat is lost through one's head?

10. In seismological circles, what is the name of the scale for describing the amount of seismic energy released by an earthquake?

Quiz 24 Answers
Measurements

1. A British hundredweight (also known as a long hundred weight) equals 112 pounds.

2. In Britain, France, and Germany a billion is not a thousand million (as in the United States) but a million million (a trillion in the United States). The U.S. million in those countries is called a milliard.

3. Lumber known as a 2×4 (two by four) is not 2 by 4 inches but 1½ by 3½ inches. When the board is first sawed from the log, it's a true 2×4, but the drying process and the planing of the board reduce it to the finished 1½- by 3½-inch size.

4. The U.S. coin that is worth 1/100 of a dollar is officially called a cent, not a penny.

5. Contrary to popular opinion, people do not use only 10 percent of their brains but much more. In fact, imaging studies have shown that no area of the brain is completely inactive. Further, when almost any area of the brain is damaged, it has specific and lasting effects on mental and behavioral capabilities.

6. Relative humidity is not the actual amount of water in a given volume of air, which is absolute humidity, but the percentage of water in the air in relation to the amount of water the air can hold at a given temperature.

On a cold day, relative humidity of a given area may be 30 percent, and yet the air may contain below 1 percent water.

7. A ten-gallon hat holds about three quarters of a gallon.

8. A pound of feathers weighs more than a pound of gold because feathers are measured by avoirdupois weight, according to which a pound is sixteen ounces, and gold is measured by troy weight, according to which a pound is twelve ounces.

9. Even though many believe that a person will lose 40 to 45 percent of body heat through the head, heat loss from the head is proportional to the size of the individual. The figures 40 to 45 percent were given in a poorly researched military study and were expressed, for example, in the 1970 *United States Army Survival Manual*.

10. The answer is not the Richter scale, which has been superseded by the Moment Magnitude Scale (MMS), devised in 1979 by seismologists Hiroo Kanamori and Tom Hanks (different guy) of the California Institute of Technology. The scientists found the Richter scale unsatisfactory because it measures only the strength of the shock waves, which don't fully reflect an earthquake's impact. Large earthquakes can have the same score on the Richter scale but cause sharply different degrees of devastation. Instead of measuring the seismic waves or vibration as experienced 373 miles away, the MMS expresses the energy released by an earthquake, multiplying the distance of the slip between the two parts of the fault by the total area affected. The MMS yields values that make sense when compared to those of the Richter scale. Further, both scales are logarithmic; a two-point increase, for example, means a hundred times more power.

Quiz 25
Language/Initials/ Mottos

1. What does *SOS*, the emergency distress signal, stand for?

2. What does the *S* in *Harry S. Truman* stand for?

3. "Neither snow, nor rain, nor heat, nor gloom of night stays these couriers from the swift completion of their appointed rounds" is whose motto?

4. Where does the expression "His name is mud" originate?

5. When was the English word *pig* first used as a pejorative for a police officer?

6. Spell the English word expressing a unit for the relative purity of gold.

7. What's the difference in the meaning between *flammable* and *inflammable*?

8. Whose official motto is *e pluribus unum* ("out of many, one")?

9. What is *corpus delicti*?

10. In Old English, the word *with* meant what?

11. Of Yiddish, Greek, Finnish, Czech, and Armenian, which language isn't Indo-European?

12. How should one pronounce *primer* in the sense of "an introductory book to teach reading" or "a short book presenting the basics of some discipline"?

13. What does *CISCO* stand for?

14. What's unusual about the word *rhythms*?

15. What is the source of the English word *arctic*?

16. What, if anything, is incorrect about the expression "is comprised of"?

17. How should one pronounce *Gallaudet* in Gallaudet University, the university for the deaf and hard-of-hearing in Washington, DC?

18. What does the Latin abbreviation *i.e.* mean?

19. How do the Cherokee pronounce *Cherokee*?

20. What is the origin of the word *sincere*?

Quiz 25 Answers
Language/Initials/Mottos

1. *SOS* stands for nothing but was chosen because of the ease with which it can be expressed in Morse code (three dots, three dashes, three dots).

2. The *S* in Harry S. Truman's name stands for nothing; technically, *S* was President Truman's middle name. According to President Truman, his parents could not agree whether he should be named after Anderson *Shipp* Truman or *Solomon* Young, his grandfathers. Some people argue, logically speaking, that the *S* should not have a period after it, though some guides to usage assert that convention calls for a period. Truman's full name was generally rendered as *Harry S. Truman*, and he did use letterhead with a period after the *S*.

3. The motto about braving the snow and rain is not the official motto of the U.S. Postal Service, which has no official motto. The words are a paraphrase of the motto written by the Greek historian Herodotus, who was describing Persia's mounted postal couriers of the fifth century BCE. The words are, however, associated with the U.S. Postal Service and are inscribed over the entrance to New York City's General Post Office at Eighth Avenue and Thirty-Third Street.

4. "His name is mud" does not come from the name of the physician who set assassin John Wilkes Booth's broken bones, Dr. Samuel Mudd, who was, by the way, found guilty of conspiring to assassinate Lincoln and sent to prison. The expression dates back to the 1820s, when the word *mud* could describe a dull fellow or a fool.

5. The word *pig* was not first used in the 1960s as a pejorative to describe the police. According to lexicographer Eric Partridge, during the early nineteenth century, *pig* came to be applied mainly to plainclothesmen in London. Note that, in other languages, long before the nineteenth century, some police were called *pigs*, as when the children of Israel condemned the Roman police authorities.

6. The word describing the relative purity of gold is not *carat*, which describes a unit of weight for measuring precious stones and gems, but *karat*. A metric carat, by the way, is 0.2 grams, making a five-carat ruby weigh one gram. *Karat* expresses the relative purity of gold. Pure gold is assumed to have twenty-four parts or karats of gold. Fourteen-karat gold contains fourteen parts gold and ten parts alloy.

7. There is no difference in meaning between *flammable* and *inflammable*, because both describe what can be easily set on fire. *Inflammable* is from the Latin *inflammare* and later from the Old English *enflamen*, meaning "to flame or burn."

8. *E pluribus unum* is not the official motto of the United States, which *used* to have that slogan as a motto, but is instead the motto of the Portuguese football club Sport Lisboa e Benfica, often abbreviated to Benfica. As noted, *E pluribus unum* used to be the national motto of the United States, but it was replaced by "In God we trust" in 1956.

9. *Corpus delicti* (literally, "body of crime") refers to the legal principle that a crime must be proved to have occurred before a person can be convicted of committing the crime. For example, no one can be properly convicted of larceny unless it can be proved that property was stolen. Similarly, someone cannot be properly convicted of arson unless it can be proved a criminal act resulted in the burning of property. In a murder case, the *corpus delicti* can include the corpse, but only a few jurisdictions require the actual production of a corpse to convict people of murder. The British serial killer John George Haigh, who murdered six persons in the 1940s, said that he decided to destroy the bodies of his victims with sulfuric acid because he believed—mistakenly—that convicting an accused of murder requires a body. Haigh had misinterpreted the Latin word *corpus* as designating a literal body rather than a figurative one.

10. In Old English the word *with* meant "against," as in "to fight with."

11. Of the languages listed the only one that is not Indo-European is Finnish (or Suomi), which is a member of the Finno-Ugric languages, which also include Estonian and Hungarian.

12. The word *primer* in the sense described is pronounced *prĭm-er* and has a short *i*, as in the world *rim*.

13. *CISCO* (the name of the corporation) is not an acronym but an abbreviated form of "San Francisco." It was originally written as "cisco."

14. *Rhythms* is reportedly the longest English word without an A, E, I, O, or U.

15. *Arctic* comes from the ancient Greek word for "bear," *arktos*, because the constellation Ursa Major, the Great Bear, lies in the northern sky. Note that the word *arctoid* is a synonym for "ursine" ("pertaining to bears").

16. *Comprise* means "contains" or "includes," as in "the whole comprises its parts"; consequently, it makes sense to say, "the organization is composed of several divisions," but "the organization comprises several divisions." The expression *is comprised of* makes no more sense than the expression *is included of.*

17. *Gallaudet* (as in Gallaudet University) is not pronounced *Gal-yoo-det* but *Gal-luh-det*.

18. The abbreviation *i.e.* (Latin for *id est*) means not "for example" (e.g.) but "that is."

19. Cherokee people don't pronounce *Cherokee* in their tongue because Cherokee speech has no *ch* or *r* sound. The correct spelling and pronunciation is *Tsalagi*. The word *Cherokee* is a Creek Indian word meaning "people with another language." Cherokee people prefer to call themselves *Aniyounwiya*, which means "the principal people."

20. The *Oxford English Dictionary* and most scholars reject the old explanation that *sincere* comes from Latin sine ("without") and cera ("wax"); rather *sincere* comes from the Latin *sincerus* ("clean," "pure," "sound"). The story about the wax appears to be folk etymology. According to one popular story, dishonest Roman or Greek sculptors would cover flaws in their works with wax to deceive viewers. From that practice, sculpture "without wax" implied honesty in perfection. Regardless of whether that artistic practice existed, most scholars reject the implied explanation of the origin of *sincere*.

World History

1. The trenches on the Western Front of World War I stretched from the frontier of Switzerland to what English body of water?

2. How many years was the Hundred Years' War between England and France?

3. What nationality was Cleopatra?

4. Who was the first person to fly nonstop across the Atlantic Ocean?

5. Where was Saint Patrick born?

6. What literature inspired Mohandas Gandhi to practice passive resistance against the British rulers of India?

7. What is the significance of Cinco de Mayo (May 5) in Mexico?

8. Where did Marco Polo come from?

9. During what war was napalm first used?

10. What kind of animal most often received the UK's Dickin Medal for animal gallantry between 1943 and 1949?

11. Compared to the height of most men of his time and place, what's true about Napoleon's height?

12. What object killed most British sailors in eighteenth-century sea battles?

13. What shape did Columbus think the Earth was?

14. In what building was Julius Caesar killed?

15. What device did medieval knights use on their wives to keep them faithful as the knights left for the Holy Lands on the Crusades?

16. Why were the followers of King James II/VII known as Jacobites?

17. What did King John do to the Magna Carta in 1215?

18. In what war were Molotov cocktails first used?

19. Who erected the obelisks known as Cleopatra's Needles?

20. Who first proposed the French defensive structure called the Maginot Line?

21. Who was the last Führer of Nazi Germany?

Quiz 26 Answers
World History

1. The trenches on the Western Front stretched from the frontier of Switzerland not to the English Channel but to the coast of the North Sea. Much of the British war effort was aimed at preventing the Germans from reaching the English Channel.

2. The Hundred Years' War lasted 116 years. On May 24, 1337, French King Philip VI started the war between England and France by taking over the English duchy of Guienne. Then, in October 1337, English King Edward III, whose mother was the sister of three French kings, formally claimed the French throne and sent troops to Normandy. In 1453, after 116 years, the series of conflicts ended, as the French finally expelled the British from Guienne.

3. Cleopatra was not Egyptian but part Macedonian, part Greek, and part Persian. Although she was the eldest daughter of Egyptian king Ptolemy XIII and ruler of Egypt during the time of Julius Caesar, Cleopatra was not Egyptian.

4. The first person to fly nonstop across the Atlantic Ocean was not Charles Lindberg, who, in 1927, became the first person to fly *solo* across the Atlantic Ocean. The first aviators to fly nonstop over the Atlantic Ocean were Captain John Alcock and his copilot Arthur Whitten Brown, two British aviators who, in 1919, flew a twin-engine Vicker Vimy nonstop from Newfoundland, Canada, to Clifden, Ireland.

5. Saint Patrick was not born in Ireland, of which he is the patron saint, but in England, where he spent much of his early life.

6. The literature that first inspired Mohandas Gandhi to practice passive resistance was not Henry David Thoreau's essay "Civil Disobedience" but the New Testament, the *Bhagavad Gita*, and Leo Tolstoy's 1899 novel *Resurrection*. Note that Gandhi first used passive resistance in 1906 in a protest against the Indian Registration Ordinance of South Africa and did not read Thoreau's "Civil Disobedience" until 1907.

7. Cinco de Mayo isn't Mexico's Independence Day, which is on September 16, but instead is a regional holiday celebrated primarily in the state of Puebla, commemorating the Mexican victory over the French in the Battle of Puebla.

8. Marco Polo was not from Venice but from Korcula, Croatia, which was a protectorate of Venice.

9. Napalm was first used not in the Vietnam War but in World War II, during the bombing of Tokyo. On March 9, 1945, General Curtis LeMay ordered U.S. bombers to drop almost two thousand tons of napalm bombs on Tokyo.

10. Carrier pigeons received thirty-two of the fifty-four Dickin Medals between 1943 and 1949. The medal, awarded for conspicuous gallantry and devotion to duty in service to British Commonwealth armed forces or civil emergency services, was also awarded to eighteen dogs, three horses, and one cat to acknowledge actions during World War II. After the war, the medal was officially replaced with the nonmilitary Silver Medal, also awarded by the UK's veterinary charity, People's Dispensary for Sick Animals (PDSA), founded by Maria Dickin.

11. Napoleon was slightly taller than the average Frenchman of his day. In 1821, shortly before his death, Napoleon was recorded at 5 feet, 2 inches *in French feet*, which correlates to a measurement of 5 feet, 6½ inches *in imperial feet*, making Napoleon's height slightly above average for his time and place. By the way, his being called the Little Corporal didn't relate to his height but was a term of affection alluding to his camaraderie with ordinary soldiers.

12. Most sailors killed in battle weren't killed by contact from cannon balls but from splintered wood flying around decks at high speeds caused by the cannon balls.

13. Columbus thought of Earth as pear shaped.

14. Julius Caesar was not killed in the Capitol despite what William Shakespeare and many other people have thought but was killed near the statue of Pompey in a hall where the Senate sometimes met. The Senate House was in a different place from the Capitol.

15. The belief that chastity belts were used during the Crusades is a modern myth. In fact, there is no credible evidence that chastity belts existed before the fifteenth century—more than a century after the last Crusade. The actual use, if any, of medieval chastity belts would have been extremely limited because the metal working then would have made it difficult to fashion a belt safe for long-term wear. The first known drawing of a chastity belt occurs in Konrad Kyeser's *Bellifortis*, a fifteenth-century book on contemporary military equipment. The book features an illustration of the "hard iron breeches" worn by Florentine women. Because the diagram shows the key, some scholars think that it was the lady and not the knight who controlled access to the device. In museum collections, most "medieval" chastity belts have been removed as probably inauthentic. Often objects advertised as medieval chastity belts were manufactured in Germany in the nineteenth century. During that time, there was an upsurge in the sale of chastity belts, but those belts were designed to prevent males from masturbating, widely regarded as harmful. Ironically, chastity belts sold in modern Western countries today are typically used in sex play.

16. Supporters of King James II/VII were called Jacobites because of the Latin word for "James" (*Jacobus*). By the way, James II was thus known when he was king of England and Ireland; he was known as James VII when he was king of Scotland.

17. King John did not sign the Magna Carta but marked the document with his seal. Some historians doubt whether the king could even write.

18. The expression *Molotov cocktail* and its referent did not originate in World War II; rather, according to Veikko

Väänänen, in the Finnish scholarly journal *Neuphilologis-che Mitteilungen* (November 4, 1977), the Finns invented and named the Molotov cocktail at some point during the 1939 to 1940 Finnish-Russian War.

19. Thothmes III erected Cleopatra's Needles.

20. The person who first proposed the French defensive structure called the Maginot Line was not André Maginot, the French minister of war in 1929 who hastened the construction of the fortification, but rather Paul Painlevé, a French mathematician who was twice prime minister of the French Third Republic.

21. The last Führer of Nazi Germany was not Hitler but Karl Dönitz, chief naval commander, appointed Führer by Hitler in late April 1945. Retaining power for twenty-three days, Dönitz led Germany during the completion of the Baltic sealift, in which more than two million Germans were removed from the eastern districts of Germany before the Russian occupation. Dönitz received a ten-year sentence at the Nuremberg trials. After serving time in Spandau prison, he lived in what was West Germany until he died in 1980 at the age of eighty-nine.

Quiz 27

Famous People

1. Generally speaking, how good a student was Einstein?

2. Besides painting and describing birds, what other bird-related activities did James Audubon enjoy?

3. How did the pop singer Cass Elliot die?

4. From what law school did the famous lawyer Clarence Darrow graduate?

5. Of Aunt Jemima, Sara Lee, and Betty Crocker, which two characters were inspired by real people?

6. Of presidents John F. Kennedy, Lyndon Baines Johnson, Richard M. Nixon, Gerald R. Ford, and James Earl Carter, who was the first to be born in a hospital?

7. As of 2009, who was the only U.S. president to be head of a labor union?

8. Who was the first U.S. president to have his inauguration televised?

9. Who was the first U.S. president to speak live on radio?

10. The first U.S. ex-president to fly in an airplane flew in which year: 1910, 1933, or 1944?

11. J. S. Bach was, in his time, most famous for what activity?

12. What happened to actress Jayne Mansfield's head when she was killed in a car accident on June 29, 1967?

13. What is the inscription on W. C. Fields's grave at Forest Lawn Cemetery in Glendale, California?

14. In what wars or conflicts did Ernest Hemingway fight?

15. Who discovered gold in 1848, sparking the California Gold Rush?

16. What's the name of the Missouri town where Mark Twain was born?

Quiz 27 Answers
Famous People

1. Einstein was an excellent student. Yes, he began to speak later than the average child, but when he did begin to speak, he spoke in complete sentences. He was earning top grades and doing physics and calculus by his early teens. True, Einstein happened to fail a college entrance exam, but he was two years younger than the average applicant and earned a brilliant score in science and math. He failed the exam because of one subject—namely, French. After he brushed up on the humanities, Einstein passed the exam and was admitted the following year.

2. Besides painting and describing birds, James Audubon spent a good deal of time killing them. He would kill more birds in a week than a duck hunter would kill in a whole season. He packed a rifle along with his palette and brushes. Quite the hunter and outdoorsman, he is said to have shot as many as a hundred birds a day.

3. The pop singer Cass Elliot did not die by choking on a sandwich but by having a heart attack.

4. Clarence Darrow never graduated from law school, though he studied law for a year at the University of Michigan. He was legally able to take the bar without having graduated.

5. Even though *Aunt Jemima* wasn't her real name and she didn't invent the pancake formula, the person behind the icon Aunt Jemima was real—Nancy Green, who had been born a slave in 1834. An excellent cook known for her warmth, she was discovered at age fifty-nine by the pancake people, who called her Aunt Jemima. At the Chicago World's Fair of 1893, she and the pancakes she represented attracted huge crowds. After the World's Fair, the pancake formula sold like, well, hotcakes, making the product (and Nancy Green's image) famous.

Sara Lee was also inspired by a real person: the daughter of bakery entrepreneur Charlie Lubin, who put her name on cheesecakes when she was only eight years old. In 1956, Lubin sold his business to Consolidated Foods and worked there as an executive for many years. In 1985, Consolidated Foods changed its name to the Sara Lee Corporation. Although the person Sara Lee never had a management position in the company, she appeared in some ads and promotions and has been a philanthropist supporting education and the advancement of girls and women in science.

Betty Crocker, a persona for General Mills since the 1920s, is quite fictitious. The surname Crocker was that of a company executive; her signature was that of a company secretary; and her radio voices were those of different actresses. In the 1930s, Betty Crocker acquired her face, a composite of several employees at General Mills. Even though Betty Crocker wasn't real, she had the distinction of being rated one of the most famous women in America.

6. Of those listed and supposedly all other American

presidents, the first one to be born in a hospital was President James Earl Carter.

7. As of 2009, the only U.S. president to be head of a labor union was Ronald Reagan, who was president of the Screen Actor's Guild.

8. The first U.S. president to have an inauguration televised was President Truman on January 20, 1949.

9. The first U.S. president to speak live on radio was not FDR but Warren Harding.

10. The first U.S. ex-president to fly in an airplane flew in 1910, the year Theodore Roosevelt flew as a passenger in a four-minute flight in one of the early Wright biplanes. The first sitting U.S. president to fly was FDR in 1943.

11. J. S. Bach was most famous in his day not for composing music but for playing the organ and for having extraordinary knowledge of the instrument. It took nearly a century for him to gain a reputation for his compositions, many of which were seldom performed in his day. One obituary read: "Our Bach was the greatest organ and clavier player who ever lived."

12. Jayne Mansfield was not decapitated, notwithstanding rumors to the contrary. According to the New Orleans Certificate of Death, the immediate cause of death was a crushed skull with "avulsion of cranium and brain." In other words, the top of her skull and brain were torn or sliced away from the rest of her head.

13. The inscription on W. C. Fields's grave is not "On the whole, I'd rather be in Philadelphia," but simply, "W. C. Fields, 1880–1946." Fields, though, did poke fun at Philadelphia in a 1925 *Vanity Fair* article, in which he proposed that his epitaph should read, "Here lies W. C. Fields, I would rather be living in Philadelphia."

14. Ernest Hemingway was not a soldier in any war. When Hemingway tried to join the army during World War I, he was rejected because of his poor vision. He then decided to join the Red Cross as an ambulance driver and was sent overseas. When delivering candy and cigarettes to Italian soldiers in 1918, he was severely wounded by fragments from an Austrian mortar shell, causing him to spend several months recuperating in a hospital. After his hospital stay, he returned to his hometown of Oak Park, Illinois, where he was treated as a war hero. In Oak Park, he stayed with his parents and spoke to civic groups about his war experiences. During the next decades of his life, he was a civilian correspondent in the Greco-Turkish War, the Spanish Civil War, and World War II. Again, although no one disputes Hemingway's courage and knowledge of war, he never served as a soldier in war.

15. The person who discovered gold in 1848, sparking the California Gold Rush, was not John Sutter, although gold was found on his property. Sutter's carpenter, in fact, discovered the gold while building a sawmill on the American River. Squatters had moved in and taken over Sutter's land after Sutter's workers had quit looking for gold. Sutter did not become rich from the discovery of the gold because he, though born in Europe, had become a Mexican citizen, and Mexico had ceded California to the United States. Because of the squatters and the cession of California to the United States, Sutter had only a questionable title to his fifty thousand acres under U.S. law. In fact, he went bankrupt in 1852 and lived off a small California pension until he died.

16. Mark Twain's birthplace was not Hannibal, Missouri (where he grew up), but Florida, Missouri.

SELECTED BIBLIOGRAPHY

Adams, Cecil. *More of the Straight Dope*. New York: Ballantine, 1988.

———. *Return of the Straight Dope*. New York: Ballantine, 1994.

The American Heritage Dictionary of the English Language, 3rd ed. Boston: Houghton Mifflin, 1992.

Boller, Paul F. Jr. *Not So!: Popular Myths About America from Columbus to Clinton*. New York: Oxford University Press, 1995.

Brasch, R. *Mistakes, Misnomers and Misconceptions*. Sydney: Fontana Books, 1983.

Burnam, Tom. *The Dictionary of Misinformation*. New York: Perennial Library, 1986.

———. *More Misinformation*. New York: Ballantine, 1980.

Del Re, Gerald. *The Whole Truth: A Compendium of Myths, Mistakes, and Misconceptions*. New York: Random House, 2004.

Dickson, Paul. *Labels for Locals: What to Call People from Abilene to Zimbabwe*. Springfield, Mass.: Merriam-Webster, 1997.

Diefendorf, David. *Amazing . . . But False!* New York: Sterling, 2007.

Evans, Rod L. *The Artful Nuance: A Refined Guide to Imperfectly Understood Words in the English Language*. New York: Perigee, 2009.

Grambs, David. *Did I Say Something Wrong?* New York: Plume, 1993.

Green, Joey. *Contrary to Popular Belief*. New York: Broadway Books, 2005.

Green, John, Maggie Kourth, Chris Connally, and Christopher Smith. *Mental Floss: What's the Difference?* New York: Collins, 2006.

Johnsen, Ferris. *The Encyclopedia of Popular Misconceptions: The Ultimate Debunker's Guide to Widely Accepted Fallacies*. New York: Citadel, 1994.

Keyes, Ralph. *Nice Guys Finish Seventh: False Phrases, Spurious Sayings, and Familiar Misquotations*. New York: HarperCollins, 1992.

———. *The Quote Verifier: Who Said What, Where, and When*. New York: St. Martin's Griffin, 2006.

Knowles, Elizabeth. *What They Didn't Say: A Book of Misquotations*. New York: Oxford University Press, 2006.

Lloyd, John, and John Mitchinson. *The Book of General Ignorance: Everything You Think You Know Is Wrong*. New York: Harmony Books, 2006.

Moore, Edwin. *Lemmings Don't Leap: 180 Myths, Misconceptions and Urban Legends Exploded*. Edinburgh: Chambers, 2007.

Morris, Evan. *From Altoids to Zima: The Surprising Stories Behind 125 Brand Names*. New York: Fireside, 2004.

Nobleman, Marc Tyler. *What's the Difference?* New York: Barnes & Noble, 2005.

Phelps, Barry. *You Don't Say! The Dictionary of Misquotations*. London: Macmillan, 1995.

Room, Adrian. *Dictionary of Confusable Words*. Chicago: Fitzroy Dearborn Publishers, 2000.

Rosenbloom, Joseph. *Polar Bears Like It Hot: A Guide to Popular Misconceptions*. New York: Sterling, 1980.

Rovin, Jeff. *What's the Difference? A Compendium of Commonly Confused and Misused Words*. New York: Ballantine, 1994.

Tuleja, Tad. *Curious Customs: The Stories Behind 296 Popular American Rituals*. New York: Galahad Books, 1999.

———. *Fabulous Fallacies: More Than 300 Popular Beliefs That Are Not True*. New York: Harmony Books, 1982.

Urdang, Laurence. *The Dictionary of Confusable Words*. New York: Ballantine, 1988.

Varasdi, J. Allen. *Myth Information*. New York: Ballantine, 1989.

Webber, Elizabeth, and Mike Feinsilber. *Merriam-Webster's Dictionary of Allusions*. Springfield, Mass.: Merriam-Webster, 1999.

The World Almanac and Book of Facts 2009. Pleasantville, N.Y.: Reader's Digest, 2009.

Zotti, Ed. *Know It All! The Fun Stuff You Never Learned in School*. New York: Ballantine, 1993.

Rod L. Evans, Ph.D., teaches philosophy at Old Dominion University in Norfolk, Virginia. He is the author or coauthor of sixteen books, including *The Gilded Tongue*, *The Right Words*, *Getting Your Words' Worth*, *Every Good Boy Deserves Fudge: The Book of Mnemonic Devices*, and *The Artful Nuance: A Refined Guide to Imperfectly Understood Words in the English Language*.